ECONOMETRICS
AN INTRODUCTORY ANALYSIS

ECONOMETRICS
AN INTRODUCTORY ANALYSIS

Teh-wei Hu

Professor of Economics
The Pennsylvania State University

University Park Press
Baltimore · London · Tokyo

UNIVERSITY PARK PRESS
Chamber of Commerce Building
Baltimore, Maryland 21202

Library of Congress Cataloging in Publication Data

Hu, Teh-wei.
  Econometrics: an introductory analysis.

  Bibliography: p.
  1. Econometrics. I. Title.
HB139.H8   658.4'033   73-1214
ISBN 0-8391-0706-4

PREFACE

This book provides a self-contained development and explanation of econometric methods for students and researchers who wish to understand and use econometrics but lack sufficient background in matrix algebra. For such students, matrix algebra often becomes a barrier to understanding econometrics. If elementary mathematics can be used to introduce econometrics, it seems unnecessary to rely on matrix algebra at this level. Thus the most important feature of this book is its step-by-step use of elementary mathematics to explain econometric methods, problems, and empirical examples.

The prerequisites for a course based on this book include one course in elementary statistics and a solid background in high school algebra. Chapter 2 reviews basic concepts and results of statistical inference. Chapter 3, which is devoted to the formulation and estimation of a single-equation regression model, is followed by a discussion of various functional forms in a regression model in Chapter 4. The problems of estimating single-equation regression models are discussed in Chapter 5; Chapter 6 deals with the applications of such models. Chapter 7 is devoted to a simultaneous equation model which includes the problems of identification, estimation, and application.

This book, of course, reflects my views on presenting econometrics. Naturally, these have been influenced by associations with my teachers, colleagues, and students. I would like to acknowledge my debt to my former teachers in econometrics, especially Arthur S. Goldberger, Harold Watts, and Arnold Zellner who have inspired and disciplined my interest.

A preliminary version of this book has been used at The Pennsylvania State University since 1967. I am grateful to Robert Tinney, who used the manuscript in his introductory econometrics class. My thanks to Milton Hallberg and Maw Lin Lee, who read early versions of Chapters

2 and 3, to Juan-shan Lee, who went over the entire manuscript, and to James Knowles, whose comments were extremely useful in the preparation of the final text. I am especially grateful to Ernst W. Stromsdorfer for constructively reading and correcting the entire manuscript. Of course, the final responsibility for any errors and defects in the text is mine.

I am also indebted to the Literary Executor of the late Sir Ronald A. Fisher, F.R.S., to Dr. Frank Yates, F.R.S., and to Oliver & Boyd, Edinburgh, for permission to reprint Table B-2 from their book *Statistical Tables for Biological, Agricultural and Medical Research*

Finally, I wish to thank my family. Their contribution, the most important by far, makes it all worthwhile.

Teh-wei Hu

CONTENTS

Contents

1

INTRODUCTION

1.1 Nature of Econometrics

Econometrics is a branch of economics that uses mathematical and statistical tools to analyze economic phenomena. The most commonly used statistical tool for measuring economic relationships is regression analysis, which is the concern of this book.

The objective of econometrics is to give empirical content to economic theory. In other words, econometrics is primarily concerned with quantitative measurement, prediction of economic phenomena, and testing hypotheses about economic phenomena. For example, if we are interested in knowing the price and income elasticities of the demand for automobiles or the shape of a demand curve for automobiles, we can collect relevant data and estimate this economic parameter by econometric techniques. Furthermore, with the estimated demand elasticity with respect to the price of automobiles we can test an economic hypothesis; for instance, whether the price elasticity of demand for automobiles is equal to unity. As we have learned in economics, this information can provide an understanding of consumer behavior. Other economic relationships can also be estimated by econometrics; examples are the supply function, the production function, the cost function, the consumption function, and all similar relationships in the analysis of economic theory.

An econometric study can be summarized by the following steps:

1. mathematical formulation of economic theories;
2. establishment of hypotheses about economic, institutional, or technological phenomena;
3. model construction with a view of statistical measurement and testing;
4. data collection;

5. statistical estimation; and
6. statistical inference relating economic theory to empirical analysis.

The statistical methods are developed primarily for
the biological and physical sciences where data are drawn
from experiments. However, the data in econometric
study are drawn from the actual outcomes of the economic
process and not from experimental observations. Therefore one of the tasks for the econometrician is to find or
modify the statistical method to be used for economic data.

Another difficulty involved in econometrics is that
economic theory specifies exact functional relationships
among its variables. In reality the measurement of the
functional relationships among its variables is not exact.
For instance, a demand function may be $q = a + bp$, where
q is quantity demanded for a given commodity and p is
price of the commodity. If we plot the observed quantity-
demanded data against the price data of a certain commodity, we find that all the points are neither on a straight line
nor on a smooth curve. Therefore, we have to introduce a
random disturbance u in the demand function; that is,
$q = a + bp + u$. This random disturbance may be positive
or negative, but it has 0 value on the average. Introducing
a random disturbance in the equation allows for individual
deviation from the exact relationship. In fact one of the
most important topics in econometrics is the nature of random disturbances in econometric study. Econometrics
provides a bridge between the exact relationships of economic theory and the random phenomena of economic
facts.

1.2   Scope of Book

The discussions above imply that there are two aspects in econometrics, one consisting of mathematical and
statistical treatment of techniques used in econometrics,
and the other consisting of applications of these tools to
the economic behavior. This book is devoted to both of
these aspects, although it emphasizes the technical aspects.

Both theoretical discussions of econometrics and empirical econometric studies by various economic topics are

presented in this book. In Chapter 2 the basic concepts and results of statistical inference are presented; this chapter provides a brief review of statistical inference and a convenient reference for subsequent chapters. Chapter 3 is devoted to the formulation and estimation of a single-equation regression model. We discuss various functional forms in a regression model in Chapter 4. Two separate sections on dummy variables and qualitative dependent variables are also included in Chapter 4. In Chapter 5 the problems of estimating single-equation regression models are discussed. Chapter 6 introduces the applications of a single-equation regression model, to teach students to appreciate and understand econometric investigations in a particular problem. Examples are chosen from the classical works of each aspect of economic topics. Finally, in Chapter 7 we introduce a simultaneous-equation model. The problems of identification, estimation, and applications of simultaneous-equation models are discussed.

2

REVIEW OF STATISTICAL INFERENCE

2.1 Probability

Statistical inference, a basic tool in the field of econometrics, is based on the laws of probability. Therefore, in this section we discuss the elements of probability theory so that we can understand the implications of statistical inference and econometric methods.

Since we are interested in the application of statistical inference to econometrics rather than the statistical theory itself, this chapter is presented as a summary of statistical inference.

2.1.1 Basic Concepts

The word *probability* is often considered to mean uncertainty or chance in our daily life. Probability is commonly thought of as an event that represents the chances of the particular event occurring. An event is defined as a possible outcome of the experiment. The classical example of probability is tossing a coin. If we toss a fair coin with no special care, we can predict that the chance of getting a head or a tail on a toss is about $\frac{1}{2}$. In this case the event can be considered as the outcome of a head or a tail. The probability of either of these two outcomes is 0.50.

The probability of event A, say $p(A)$, can be between 0 and 1. In most cases it will be between these two values. Therefore, it follows that

$$0 \leqslant p(A) \leqslant 1. \qquad (2\text{-}1)$$

This can be illustrated again by the example of the coin tossing. We cannot observe more tails than the total number of tossings, nor can we have fewer than 0 outcomes of tails. If the probability of an event is equal to 1, then we can say the event will occur with certainty. If the probability of an event is close to 0, then the occurrence of the event is close to impossible.

2.1.2 Addition Rule and Multiplication Rule

Sometimes we may be interested not only in the probability of an event, say A, but also in the probability of two events, say A and B, or three events A, B, and C. There are two basic rules for the calculation of such probabilities.

Addition Rule: If two events A and B are mutually exclusive (cannot occur together), then the probability of either A or B is the sum of their separate probabilities. So we have

$$p(A \text{ or } B) = p(A) + p(B). \tag{2-2}$$

The Venn diagram in Figure 2-1(a) shows that event A and event B have no overlapping. The same rule applies to three events. The probability of either A or B or C is

$$p(A \text{ or } B \text{ or } C) = p(A) + p(B) + p(C). \tag{2-3}$$

If A and B are not mutually exclusive, the outcome of either A or B means the outcome of either A or B or both A and B. The probability of either A or B (or both) is given by

$$p(A \text{ or } B) = p(A) + p(B) - p(A \text{ and } B). \tag{2-4}$$

Figure 2-1(b) illustrates the nonmutually exclusive case that there is an overlapping area between event A and event B. Equation (2-4) is a general formula for the law of addition, whereas Equation (2-2) is a special case of Equation (2-4) when $p(A \text{ and } B) = 0$.

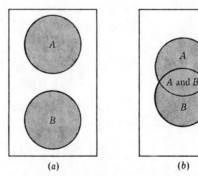

(a)   (b)

Figure 2-1 Venn diagrams. (a) A and B are mutually exclusive; (b) A and B are nonmutually exclusive.

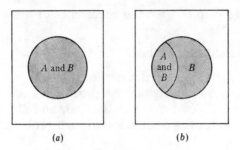

(a)   (b)

Figure 2-2 Venn diagrams. (a) A and B events occur simultaneously; (b) conditional probability of A, given B, $p(A|B)$.

Multiplication Rule: Again there are two cases. First, if event A does not depend on event B, then the probability of both A and B occurring is the product of their probabilities. Figure 2-2(a) shows this first case:

$$p(A \text{ and } B) = p(A) \cdot p(B). \qquad (2\text{-}5)$$

Second, if the outcome of A does depend on the outcome of B, then the joint outcome of A and B is the probability that B occurs multiplied by the probability of A, given that event B occurs:

$$p(A \text{ and } B) = p(B) \cdot p(A|B). \qquad (2\text{-}6)$$

The symbol $p(A|B)$ is called the conditional probability of A, given the outcome of B. A conditional probability is the probability of an event, given the condition with respect to the occurrence of other events. Based on Equation (2-6) the conditional probability of $p(A|B)$ can be expressed as

$$p(A|B) = \frac{p(A \text{ and } B)}{p(B)}. \qquad (2\text{-}7)$$

Figure 2-2(b) illustrates the case of the conditional probability, $p(A|B)$.

Comparing Equations (2-5) and (2-6), we find that if events A and B are independent of each other, then

$$p(A|B) = p(A). \qquad (2\text{-}8)$$

Equation (2-8) is a general definition of statistical independence, a very important concept in statistical inference and econometrics. We use it extensively throughout this text.

2.1.3 Sampling

A population is the totality of the elements under study. A sample is a part of a population. For example, an economist is interested in knowing about the consumption pattern of all families having an annual income of $3000. It would be very expensive and time-consuming to collect data for all such families. Therefore, he selects a part of the population (a sample) in such a way that the sample is representative of the population. To achieve this objective the economist should randomly select the sample from a proper population to ensure the representativeness of the sample. A random sample is one in which each individual in the population is equally likely to be sampled.

In general, statistical inference may be considered as methods for drawing conclusions about populations from samples. It is necessary to use probability in such conclusions because a conclusion based on a sample cannot give us complete information about the population, and therefor it cannot be made with certainty.

2.2   Random Variable

2.2.1   Notion of a Random Variable

A random variable is sometimes called a stochastic variable. It is defined as a variable whose value is determined by an experiment. For example, the outcome of the throw of a die is a random variable because it can assume the values of 1, 2, 3, 4, 5, and 6, with the particular value determined by the experiment.

For simplicity, only discrete random variables are discussed in this section. A discrete random variable is a variable that takes on only a finite number of values with probability specified in its probability function. The die-throwing example is a case of a discrete random variable. We can find

$$p(1) = \tfrac{1}{6} = p_1$$
$$p(2) = \tfrac{1}{6} = p_2$$
$$\vdots$$
$$p(6) = \tfrac{1}{6} = p_6 \ .$$

The set of the equations above is called a probability function. It can be seen that the sum of the probabilities of the total outcome is equal to unity. This follows from the addition rule for probabilities. In the die-throwing example we have

$$p_1 + p_2 + \cdots + p_6 = 6(\tfrac{1}{6}) = 1 ,$$

or in general expression,

$$\sum_{i=1}^{n} p_i = 1 \qquad i = 1, 2, \ldots, n. \qquad (2\text{-}9)$$

The symbol Σ means summation. A detailed review of the mathematics of the summation operation is presented in Appendix A.

We have so far discussed one random variable. Consider the case in which two random variables, X and Y, might occur together. The probability function of X and Y, $p(X$ and $Y)$, is called the joint probability function $p(X, Y)$. As an example, we may consider the drawing of a card from an ordinary deck of playing cards. The 52 outcomes may be classified according to suit (say X_1, X_2, X_3, and X_4) or according to determination (say Y_1, Y_2, . . . , Y_{13}). The probability of the event X_1 and Y_2, for example, is denoted as $p(X_1, Y_2)$, and the value of this joint probability is 1/52.

2.2.2 Mean and Variance

Mean and variance are two of the important characteristics of a sample or population distribution. Mean indicates the location or center of a distribution, whereas variance is a measure of the dispersion or spread of a distribution. There are two other concepts of the location of a distribution: mode and median. The mode is defined as the most frequent value in a distribution whereas the median is the value that splits the distribution into two halves. The most common measure for the center of a distribution is the mean.

The mean of a distribution is a measure of what one might expect, on the average, as a result. It is also called the mathematical expectation or expected value of a random variable. Let X_1, X_2, . . . , X_n be the possible values of the random variables with respective probabilities $p(X_1)$,

$p(X_2), \ldots, p(X_n)$. Then the mean or the mathematical expectation of X, μ, or $E(X)$ is

$$E(X) = \sum_{i=1}^{n} X_i p(X_i)$$
$$= \mu . \tag{2-10}$$

Equation (2-10) also implies that the mean is a weighted average. The weights are the probabilities with respect to its values that X can take on. The symbol $E(\ )$ is called the expected-value operator. A numerical example of computing the expected value of a random variable follows.

Values of the random variable X	Probability of $p(X_i)$	Weighted values of X $X_i p(X_i)$
0	0.25	0.00
1	0.50	0.50
2	0.25	0.50
	1.00	$E(X) = 1.00$

The immediate consequences of Equation (2-10) are the following statements.

Statement (2-1) If c is a constant, then $E(c) = c$.
We can establish this as follows:

$$E(c) = \sum_{i=1}^{n} cp(X_i)$$

$$= c \sum_{i=1}^{n} p(X_i)$$

$$= c \quad \text{since } \sum_{i=1}^{n} p(X_i) = 1.$$

Statement (2-2) If c is a constant, then $E(cX) = cE(X)$.
The proof follows:

$$E(cX) = \sum_{i=1}^{n} cX_i \, p(X_i)$$

$$= c \sum_{i=1}^{n} X_i \, p(X_i)$$

$$= cE(X).$$

Statement (2-3) If X and Y are random variables, then $E(X + Y) = E(X) + E(Y)$.

9

Review of Statistical Inference

We can establish this in the following manner:

$$E(X + Y) = \sum_{i=1}^{n} \sum_{j=1}^{n} (X_i + Y_j)\, p(X_i, Y_j)$$

$$= \sum_{i=1}^{n} \sum_{j=1}^{n} X_i\, p(X_i, Y_j) + \sum_{i=1}^{n} \sum_{j=1}^{n} Y_j\, p(X_i, Y_j)$$

$$= \sum_{i=1}^{n} X_i \sum_{j=1}^{n} p(X_i, Y_j) + \sum_{j=1}^{n} Y_j \sum_{i=1}^{n} p(X_i, Y_j)$$

$$= \sum_{i=1}^{n} X_i\, p(X_i) + \sum_{j=1}^{n} Y_j\, p(Y_j)$$

$$= E(X) + E(Y).$$

Statement (2-4) If X and Y are independent random variables, then $E(XY) = E(X)E(Y)$.

The word *independent* implies that the probability of obtaining various values of X_1 in no way depends upon the values of X_2, and vice versa. The proof of Statement (2-4) follows:

$$E(XY) = \sum_{i=1}^{n} \sum_{j=1}^{n} X_i Y_j\, p(X_i Y_j)$$

$$= \sum_{i=1}^{n} X_i\, p(X_i) \sum_{j=1}^{n} Y_j\, p(Y_j)$$

since X and Y are independent,
$$p(X_i, Y_j) = p(X_i)\, p(Y_j)$$

$$= E(X)E(Y).$$

The population mean is usually expressed as μ. The mean of sample observations with size n from a population is called the sample mean $\overline{X}$. The expected value of $\overline{X}$ is also equal to μ.

$$E(\overline{X}) = \frac{1}{n} \sum_{i=1}^{n} E(X_i)$$

$$= \frac{1}{n} \cdot nE(X) = E(X)$$

$$= \mu. \qquad (2\text{-}11)$$

A random variable can almost always take on values different from the expected value. Therefore, we need a measure of the degree to which the actual values differ from the expected values. The most common measure is the variance of distribution, $V(X)$, or σ^2,

$$V(X) = E(X - \mu)^2 = \sum_{i=1}^{n} (X_i - \mu)^2$$

$$= \sigma^2. \qquad (2\text{-}12)$$

Equation (2-12) states that the variance of a random variable X is computed as the sum of the squared deviations of the random variables from the expected value weighted by the probability of the variable. The variance is always positive, for neither squares nor probabilities are negative. A numerical example of computing the variance of the random variable follows.

Values of the random variable X	Probability of X $p(X_i)$	Deviation of X from μ $(X_i - \mu)$	Square of deviation $(X_i - \mu)^2$	Weighted squared deviation $(X_i - \mu)^2 p(X_i)$
0	0.25	-1	1	0.25
1	0.50	0	0	0.00
2	0.25	1	1	0.25
	1.00	0.00		$V(X) = 0.50 = \sigma^2$

When we consider that $X_1, X_2, \ldots, X_n$ are a sample with size n drawn from a population with population mean μ and variance σ^2, the sample variance can be defined as follows:

$$S^2 = \frac{\sum_{i=1}^{n} (X_i - \overline{X})^2}{n - 1}. \qquad (2\text{-}13)$$

In words, the sample variance is computed by dividing the sum of squares of the deviations from their sample mean by $n - 1$; that is, by 1 less than the number of values in the sample. The quantity $(n - 1)$ is called the number of degrees of freedom.

The phrase "a degree of freedom" can be illustrated in the following way. If the sum of a distribution of four values is specified as 10, any three values can be specified freely, but the fourth must be chosen so as to satisfy the restriction that the total be 10. Specifying the sum has removed one degree of freedom for values to enter the total sample observations.   In computing sample variance we need to know the sample mean. The sample mean is obtained from information in the total sample size n. This

11

uses up one degree of freedom. Hence when we compute the sample variance, we have only $(n - 1)$ degrees of freedom left.

In fact the mathematical expectation of the sample variance shown in Equation (2-13) is equal to the population variance. The proof of this statement is presented in Section 2.3.

The square root of the variance σ is called the standard deviation of the distribution. It is used as a measure of the dispersion. The immediate consequences of Equation (2-12) are the following statement.

Statement (2-5) If c is a constant, then $V(c) = 0$.
That is,

$$V(c) = E[c - E(c)]^2 = E(c - c)^2$$

$$= 0 .$$

Statement (2-6) If c is a constant, then $V(cX) = c^2 V(X)$.
The proof follows:

$$V(cX) = E[cX - E(cX)]^2 = E(cX - c\mu)^2$$

$$= c^2 E(X - \mu)^2 = c^2 V(X) .$$

Statement (2-7) If X and Y are random variables, then $V(X + Y) = V(X) + V(Y) + 2 \operatorname{Cov}(X, Y)$, where $\operatorname{Cov}(X, Y)$ is the covariance of X and Y, the product of $E[(X - E(X)) \cdot (Y - E(Y))]$.
The proof follows:

$$V(X + Y) = E[(X + Y) - E(X + Y)]^2$$

$$= E[(X - E(X)) + (Y - E(Y))]^2$$

$$= E[X - E(X)]^2 + E[Y - E(Y)]^2$$

$$+ 2E[(X - E(X)) (Y - E(Y))]$$

$$= V(X) + V(Y) + 2 \operatorname{Cov}(X, Y).$$

Statement (2-8) If X and Y are independent random variables, then $V(X + Y) = V(X) + V(Y)$, for

$$\operatorname{Cov}(X, Y) = E[(X - E(X)) (Y - E(Y))]$$

$$= E(XY) - E(X)E(Y)$$

since $E(X)$ and $E(Y)$ are constants,
by Statement (2-4)

$$= 0 .$$

Covariance is a very useful concept in econometrics. A positive value of the covariance of X and Y implies that high values of X tend to be associated with high values of Y. The relation between consumption-disposable income is an example. On the other hand, if high values of X are more frequently associated with low values of Y, the covariance of X and Y will be negative. As an example, one can think of pairs of variables such as the price and quantity demanded of a certain commodity. When X does not tend to be frequently associated with either high or low values of Y, then the covariance of X and Y tends to be 0.

Covariance is a measure of the degree to which two variables are correlated. Zero covariance implies that values of X and Y are not correlated. However, uncorrelatedness between X and Y does not mean that X and Y are independent. Although Statement (2-8) shows that when X and Y are independent, X and Y are always uncorrelated, it is possible that X and Y are dependent but have 0 covariance. For instance, variables X and Y have the following probability distribution.

X_i \ Y_j	-1	0	1
-1	0.3	0.0	0.3
1	0.0	0.4	0.0

Based on this example, we can derive the following information.

X_i	$p(X_i)$	Y_j	$p(Y_j)$
-1	0.6	-1	0.3
1	0.4	0	0.4
		1	0.3

The conditional probability of $p(X_i|Y_j)$ can be derived from Equation (2-7). The estimated probabilities are summarized below.

X_i	$p(X_i|Y = 1)$	$p(X_i|Y = 0)$	$p(X_i|Y = 1)$
-1	1(= 0.3/0.3)	0(= 0.0/0.4)	1(= 0.3/0.3)
1	0(= 0.0/0.3)	1(= 0.4/0.4)	0(= 0.0/0.3)

If X is distributed independently of Y, then $p(X_i|Y_j) = p(X_i)$. The comparison between these calculations tells us that $p(X_i|Y_j) \neq p(X_i)$. Therefore X and Y are dependent.

Review of Statistical Inference

However, the covariance of X and Y is equal to 0. This can be proved as follows:

$$\text{Cov}(X_i Y_j) = \sum_{i=1}^{2} \sum_{j=1}^{3} (X_i - \mu_x)(Y_j - \mu_j) p(X_i Y_j)$$

$$= 0.24 + 0.0 + 0.0 + 0.0 + 0.0 - 0.24$$

$$= 0.$$

The variance of the mean from a sample of size n can be computed as follows:

$$V(\overline{X}) = V\left(\frac{1}{n} \sum_{i=1}^{n} X_i\right) = \frac{1}{n^2} \sum_{i=1}^{n} V(X_i)$$

$$= \frac{1}{n^2} n V(X) = \frac{1}{n} V(X)$$

$$= \frac{\sigma^2}{n}. \tag{2-14}$$

The square root of the variance of a sample mean, $\sigma/\sqrt{n}$, is called the standard error of the mean.

2.2.3 Normal Distribution

The normal distribution can be considered as the cornerstone of modern statistical theory. It was first found in physical and biological sciences that the distribution of errors of measurement in scientific observations were closely approximated by a continuous curve, called a *normal curve*. This curve is bell-shaped. The location and shape of a normal curve are determined by its values of μ and σ. The normal distribution is symmetric about the mean; that is, the mean of the distribution is a median and also a mode of the distribution.

The normal distribution in statistics is important because a great many statistical techniques are based on the assumption that most populations have the normal distribution. Furthermore, once the assumption of normal distribution has been established, the statistical inference can be made easily.

As we know, the normal distribution is defined completely by the values of the mean and variance of the distribution. Because it is a symmetric distribution, the value of the mean determines not only the location but also the peak of the distribution. One normal distribution differs from another only in location μ or dispersion σ^2. There-fore, it would be a great convenience if we could transform all normal distributions with different values of μ and σ into a standardized normal distribution. By a theorem, a linear transformation of a normal variable is itself a normal variable. The transformation follows:

$$Z = \frac{X - \mu}{\sigma} .$$
(2-15)

The variable Z is called the standardized or normalized vari-able. A standardized variable has 0 mean and unit variance. This result can be shown by means of the rules of expecta-tion discussed in Section 2.2.2:

$$E(Z) = E\left(\frac{X - \mu}{\sigma}\right) = \frac{1}{\sigma}[E(X) - \mu]$$

$$= 0 ,$$

while

$$V(Z) = E[Z - E(Z)]^2 = E\left(\frac{X - \mu}{\sigma}\right)^2$$

$$= \frac{1}{\sigma^2} E(X - \mu)^2 \qquad \text{using Equation (2-12)}$$

$$= 1 .$$

Figure 2-3 gives us the standardized normal distribu-tion curve, with mean 0 and standard deviation 1. Table 1 of Appendix B gives the area under any part of the normal curve for the variable Z, that is, for the standard-

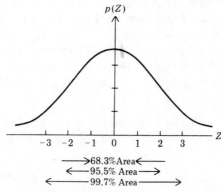

Figure 2-3   The standardized normal dis-tribution with mean zero and unit vari-ance.

ized normal variable. The total area under the curve is equal to 1.

To illustrate the use of the standardized normal distribution, the probability that Z falls between -1 and 1 standard deviations, as shown in Figure 2-3, is 0.683, or 68.3%, of the distribution. The probability that Z falls between -2 and 2 standard deviations is 0.955, or 95.5%, of the distribution. Similarly the probability that Z falls between -3 and 3 standard deviations is 0.997, or 99.7%, of the distribution.

2.2.4 Central Limit Theorem

Mathematical results tell us that if random variable X possesses a normal distribution with mean μ and standard deviation σ, then the sample mean $\overline{X}$, based on a random sample of size n, will also possess a normal distribution with mean μ and standard deviation $\sigma/\sqrt{n}$.

Suppose that the random variable X does not possess a normal distribution. What can we say about distribution of $\overline{X}$? According to a mathematical theorem, we can say that if X possesses a distribution with mean μ and standard deviation σ, then the distribution of sample mean $\overline{X}$ approaches a normal distribution with mean μ and standard deviation $\sigma/\sqrt{n}$ as the sample size n increases. This is known as the *central limit theorem*.

The central limit theorem is one of the most important theorems in statistics. This theorem justifies our efforts to study the normal distribution. It implies that, although individual variables are not normally distributed, almost regardless of the shape of the original distributions, the mean of a sample size of such variables does tend to be normally distributed. Therefore, the assumption of a normal population is often valid for $\overline{X}$ as an approximation for large samples even when the population is not normally distributed.

We have proved that $E(\overline{X}) = \mu$ and $V(\overline{X}) = \sigma^2/n$; therefore we can state that the transformed random variable

$$\frac{\overline{X} - \mu}{\sigma/\sqrt{n}} \tag{2-16}$$

is a standard normal variable with mean 0 and unit variance when n is large.

2.3 Estimation

The problems of statistical inference include the problems of estimating population parameters and testing hypotheses. Hypotheses testing is discussed in Section 2.4.

2.3.1 Desirable Properties of Estimators

Estimation refers to obtaining the value of some unknown parameters of the population distribution from the information in the sample. The particular value obtained from the observations in a sample in order to infer an unknown population parameter is called an estimate. However, an estimate is different from the concept of estimator. An estimator refers to the method of estimating a population parameter. In other words, an estimate is a specific value that an estimator takes. For example, $\overline{X}$ is called an estimator of μ if we use $\overline{X}$ to estimate μ.

Statisticians use a few criteria for the selection of desirable estimators of population parameters. A desirable estimator is often the one whose distribution is concentrated near the true parameter. Therefore, most of the criteria refer to the mean and variance of the distribution of the estimator.

Desirable properties of statistical estimators can be discussed under two conditions relating to sample size; namely, the case for a finite sample size and the case for an infinite sample size.

Suppose that μ is a true population parameter, say the population mean, while $\hat{\mu}$ is an estimate of μ. The criteria for selecting an estimator under a finite sample size are:

1. *Unbiasedness.* $\hat{\mu}$ is an unbiased estimate of μ if

$$E(\hat{\mu}) = \mu \ . \tag{2-17}$$

In other words, when the expected value of the estimator is equal to the population parameter, then the estimator is unbiased.

Unbiasedness has intuitive appeal as a property of an estimator since it indicates that if the process were repeated many times, the average of the estimates would be very close to the true population parameter. For example, Equation (2-11) has shown that the expected value of the sample mean $\overline{X}$ is the population

17

mean μ. Therefore, the sample mean is an unbiased estimate of the population mean.

As indicated in Section 2.2.2, the expected value of the sample variance, Equation (2-13), is equal to the population variance. In other words, the sample variance is also an unbiased estimator. The proof follows:

$$s^2 = \frac{1}{n-1}\left[\sum_{i=1}^{n}(X_i - \overline{X})^2\right]$$

$$= \frac{1}{n-1}\left\{\sum_{i=1}^{n}[(X_i - \mu) - (\overline{X} - \mu)]^2\right\}$$

$$= \frac{1}{n-1}\left[\sum_{i=1}^{n}(X_i - \mu)^2 - n(\overline{X} - \mu)^2\right].$$

Taking the expected value of both sides

$$E(s^2) = \frac{1}{n-1}E\left[\sum(X_i - \mu)^2 - n(\overline{X} - \mu)^2\right]$$

$$= \frac{1}{n-1}(n\sigma^2 - \sigma^2)$$

$$= \sigma^2.$$

2. *Minimum variance.* $\hat{\mu}$ is a minimum-variance estimator of μ if

$$E(\hat{\mu} - \mu)^2 \leqslant E(\hat{\hat{\mu}} - \mu)^2, \qquad (2\text{-}18)$$

where $\hat{\hat{\mu}}$ is any other estimator of μ. When an estimator $\hat{\mu}$ is unbiased and has minimum variance, it is called the best unbiased estimator of μ. In general, we prefer to choose an estimator with a sample distribution closely concentrated around the population parameter. The comparison among a set of estimators is based on the variances of these estimators, assuming that we have unbiased estimators. The smaller the variance, the more concentrated the sampling distribution around the population parameter.

The traditional criterion for a finite sample size states that $\hat{\mu}$ is a best linear unbiased estimator for μ if $\hat{\mu}$ is a linear function of the sample observations, is unbiased, and has minimum variance.

There are several properties of estimators as the sample size approaches infinity. These are often called *large-sample properties.*

1. *Asymptotic unbiasedness.* An asymptotic unbiased estimator is the estimator whose bias vanishes when the sample size is sufficiently large. Algebraically, the condition of asymptotic unbiasedness is

$$\lim_{n \to \infty} E(\hat{\mu}_{\hat{n}} - \mu) = 0, \qquad (2\text{-}19)$$

where $\lim_{n \to \infty}$ implies the limit as the sample size n approaches infinity. $\hat{\mu}_n$ is denoted as the estimator of a large sample size n.

2. *Consistency.* A consistent estimator is one whose sampling distribution collapses on the parameter as the sample size becomes sufficiently large. Mathematically, this condition can be expressed in terms of the concept of a probability limit. That is,

$$p \lim_{n \to \infty} (|\hat{\mu}_n - \mu| < c) = 1, \qquad (2\text{-}20)$$

where $p \lim_{n \to \infty}$ stands for probability limit. Equation (2-20) implies that an estimator $\hat{\mu}_{\hat{n}}$ of a parameter μ is said to be consistent if for every value of μ the probability that $\hat{\mu}_n$ differs in absolute value from μ by less than any positive number c (however small) can be made as close to 1, as the sample size increases becomes infinitely large. Therefore, Equation (2-20) can be written as

$$p \lim \hat{\mu}_n = \mu. \qquad (2\text{-}21)$$

Consistency is one of the most important asymptotic properties. It assures us that larger samples will allow us to obtain an estimator closer to a population parameter. This also implies that a consistent estimator is asymptotically unbiased. However, the converse is not true.

3. *Asymptotic efficiency.* Asymptotic efficiency is used as a relative measure. $\hat{\mu}_n$ is an asymptotically efficient estimator of μ if it is consistent and if $\hat{\mu}$ has the smallest variance among any other consistent estimators. Although the variance of a consistent estimator goes to 0 as the sample size increases, it may still be possible to obtain the one that approaches 0 fastest.

2.3.2 Point Estimation and Interval Estimation

A point estimation is a single number obtained from computations on the observed values of the random variable that serves as an estimator of the parameter. For

19

example, suppose that we wish to estimate the average weight of all college students in the United States. Let X be the random variable designating the weight for each student. A random sample of n students is drawn, and the average weight of the sample students is denoted by $\overline{X}$. If we are told that a sample of 2000 students is taken and $\overline{X}$ is 160, and if we are asked to estimate the population mean μ on the basis of this information, then such a statistic is called a *point estimator* since this is a specific value as an estimator for μ.

Unfortunately error is likely to occur when we have point estimation. This is because the sample on which the estimation is based is merely a small subset of the population. It is obvious that when the sample observations become sufficiently large, the sample estimator will be almost the same as the population parameter. However, since we are often limited in resources and time, we cannot always obtain a larger sample. To use the available information in the best possible way, the criteria discussed in the preceding section help us to choose a "good" estimator.

The two most common methods of point estimation are the *maximum-likelihood* and least-squares methods. The method of maximum-likelihood estimation involves obtaining an estimate of the population parameter that would maximize the probability of obtaining the sample actually observed. The particular value that maximizes this probability is chosen as the estimate of the parameters. The method of least squares involves choosing the value that minimizes the sum of the squares of the deviations from the chosen value. This method has been used extensively in econometrics.

An interval estimate is determined by two numbers, obtained from computations on the observed values of the random variable, that are expected to contain the true value of the parameter in their interval. Consider the distribution of $\overline{X}$ for random samples from a normal population with the mean μ and the variance σ^2. Given a certain confidence level, we can form a probability statement based on the standardized normal distribution:

$$\text{prob}\left(Z_{-\alpha/2} < \frac{\overline{X} - \mu}{\sigma/\sqrt{n}} < Z_{\alpha/2}\right) = 1 - \alpha \qquad (2\text{-}22)$$

where $1 - \alpha$ is the probability of the confidence coefficient,

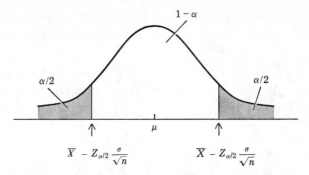

Figure 2-4 The confidence coefficient $(1 - \alpha)$ and the confidence interval.

say 95%, and $Z_{-\alpha/2}$ and $Z_{\alpha/2}$ are the values of the standardized standard deviations corresponding to $1 - \alpha$. With $1 - \alpha$ equal to 95%, $Z_{-\alpha/2}$ and $Z_{\alpha/2}$ are -1.96 and 1.96, respectively. The above inequality can be solved for μ, obtaining the equivalent inequality as follows:

$$\text{prob}\left(\overline{X} - Z_{\alpha/2}\frac{\sigma}{\sqrt{n}} < \mu < \overline{X} + Z_{\alpha/2}\frac{\sigma}{\sqrt{n}}\right) = 1 - \alpha. \quad (2\text{-}23)$$

Equation (2-23) can be illustrated by Figure 2-4.

It should be noted that population mean μ is a constant, not a variable. Equation (2-23) is a probability statement about the random variable $\overline{X}$. Therefore, it is the interval $\overline{X} - Z_{\alpha/2}\,(\sigma/\sqrt{n})$, $\overline{X} + Z_{\alpha/2}\,(\sigma/\sqrt{n})$ that varies about μ. Once the sample has been observed and $\overline{X}$ is taken, the estimated two values become a confidence interval.

The example illustrated in the point estimation also can be discussed in confidence-interval estimation. We assume that $\overline{X}$ is normal with mean μ and standard deviation $\sigma/\sqrt{n} = 5$ lb. Thus from Equation (2-23) we know that there is a 95% probability that μ will fall in the range of 150.2 to 169.8 lb:

$$\text{prob}\,[160 - 1.96(5) < \mu < 160 + 1.96(5)] = 95\%$$

or the confidence interval for μ:

$$160 \pm 9.8 = 150.2 \text{ to } 169.8.$$

2.3.3 Small-Sample Estimation: The t Distribution

In most applied problems the population standard deviation is unknown. Furthermore, the sample size is not large enough to treat the sampling distribution of $\overline{X}$ as if it were a normal distribution. In order to develop an appli-

21

cable theory for small samples it is assumed that the population from which we are sampling has roughly the shape of a normal distribution.

Recall Equation (2-16). We know that X has a normal distribution and that σ is known; thus we may standardize, obtaining

$$Z = \frac{\overline{X} - \mu}{\sigma/\sqrt{n}}.$$

If σ is unknown and if we replace σ by its estimate s, we have a new t variable, defined as

$$t = \frac{\overline{X} - \mu}{s/\sqrt{n}}, \tag{2-24}$$

where s is the sample standard deviation and n is the number of observations. The t variable resembles the standard normal variable. The shape of the t distribution is very much like that of the normal curve; it is symmetrical with respect to its mean, but there is a slightly higher probability of getting values falling into the two tails as compared with the normal distribution curve. The exact shape of the distribution depends on the size of the sample or on the degrees of freedom $n - 1$. The comparison of t and normal distributions is shown in Figure 2-5.

It appears from Figure 2-5 that the larger the number of degrees of freedom, the more the t distribution approximates the normal distribution. Hence if the number of degrees of freedom becomes as large as or larger than 30, we may use instead of t the variable Z, which is normally distributed with 0 mean and unit variance. Table 2 of Appendix B gives the calculated students' t distribution.

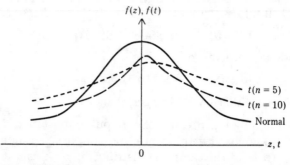

Figure 2-5 Comparison of t and normal distributions.

The t distribution is widely used in connection with problems of obtaining confidence limits for a mean, of testing hypotheses about the mean, and the difference of two means.

Confidence-interval estimation for a population mean based on a small sample with unknown population variance σ can be illustrated as follows.

We construct a random variable $(\overline{X} - \mu)/(s/\sqrt{n})$ that has a t distribution with $n - 1$ degrees of freedom. Then the estimated confidence interval of the population mean will be as follows:

$$\text{prob}\left(\overline{X} - t_{\alpha/2} \frac{s}{\sqrt{n}} < \mu < \overline{X} + t_{\alpha/2} \frac{s}{\sqrt{n}}\right) = 1 - \alpha. \quad (2\text{-}25)$$

2.3.4 Estimating the Variance: The Chi-Square Distribution

We have so far not discussed the estimation of a confidence interval for the variance. Suppose that we have estimated s^2 from a sample and that we would like to know the population variance σ^2. In Section 2.3.1 we have already shown that s^2 is an unbiased estimator of σ^2. But to estimate the confidence interval for σ^2, based on s^2, we have to rely on the chi-square distribution, or χ^2 distribution.

Consider a sample $X_1, X_2, \ldots, X_n$ taken from a normal distribution with mean μ and variance σ^2. The standardized normal variable shown by Equation (2-15) is defined as Z. Let us now construct the following statistic:

$$\chi^2 = \sum_{i=1}^{n} Z_i^2 = \sum_{i=1}^{n} \left(\frac{X - \mu}{\sigma}\right)^2. \quad (2\text{-}26)$$

The statistic χ^2 has a distribution called the chi-square distribution with n degrees of freedom. n is the number of independent standardized normal variables in Equation (2-26). When the sample size is relatively small, the χ^2 distribution becomes a positively skewed curve (tapered toward the high value). The exact shape of the distribution will depend upon the values of σ^2 and n. We show in Figure 2-6 the χ^2 distribution for 1 to 6 degrees of freedom. It is apparent from the graph that the χ^2 distribution for 6 degrees of freedom is more similar to a normal distribution than one for χ^2 with 3 degrees of freedom.

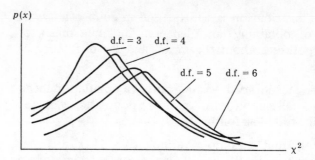

Figure 2-6 The chi-square distribution with different degrees of freedom.

We can summarize that if s^2 is the variance of a random sample of size n from the normal distribution with mean μ and variance σ^2, then $(n-1)\,s^2/\sigma^2$ has a chi-square distribution with $n-1$ degrees of freedom. The statistic can be expressed by

$$\chi^2 = \frac{(n-1)\,s^2}{\sigma^2}. \qquad (2\text{-}27)$$

The mean of a chi-square distribution is equal to the number of degrees of freedom, and the variance of the distribution is equal to twice the degrees of freedom.

The χ^2 distribution is widely used in connection with problems of testing goodness of fit, testing hypotheses about the variance of a normal distribution, and obtaining a confidence interval for the variance of a normal distribution.

We now use our familiar technique to show the method of constructing a confidence interval for σ^2. Suppose that we wish to estimate the 95% confidence interval for σ^2, based on s^2. From Equation (2-27) we find this to be

$$\text{prob}\left[\chi^2_{(n-1,\,1-\alpha/2)} < \frac{s^2\,(n-1)}{\sigma^2} < \chi^2_{(n-1,\,\alpha/2)}\right] = 95\%. $$
$$(2\text{-}28)$$

$\chi^2_{(n-1,\,1-\alpha/2)}$ is the critical value that can be obtained from the χ^2 distribution table. Solving for σ^2 we obtain the equivalent statement

$$\text{prob}\left[\frac{s^2}{(n-1)\cdot\chi^2_{(n-1,\,0.025)}} < \sigma^2 \right.$$

$$\left. < \frac{s^2}{(n-1)\cdot\chi^2_{(n-1,\,0.975)}}\right] = 95\%.$$

2.4   Hypothesis Testing

The testing of an hypothesis is designed to determine whether a given sample would reasonably come from a specified population.   There is an intimate connection between estimation and the testing of hypotheses.   For instance, testing the hypothesis that a parameter has a specified value is equivalent to computing the confidence interval for that parameter about the specified value. However, this statement is correct only when a two-tailed test is performed.

2.4.1   Procedures of Hypothesis Testing

The testing of an hypothesis involves deciding whether to accept or to reject the hypothesis. Empirical tests of hypotheses are called tests of significance. Such tests are probability tests based on sampling theory.   They are designed to determine whether a given sample could reasonably come from a specified population.

A statistical hypothesis is a statement about one or more parameters of a population or a group of populations. In testing an hypothesis a number of steps should be taken.   First, we must make an assumption about the nature of the underlying distribution of the population. Second, the hypothesis to be tested should be stated in terms of a specific parameter or parameters of the population.

For example, we may test the hypothesis that the population mean μ is equal to μ_0 against the alternative hypothesis that μ is not equal to μ_0; that is,

$$H_0 : \mu = \mu_0$$
$$H_a : \mu \neq \mu_0,$$

where μ_0 is a specific mean of the population. H_0 denotes the null hypothesis and H_a denotes the alternative hypothesis.   The null hypothesis is considered, in most cases, as the statement about the absence of any effect claimed for a certain action.

Two types of error may be made in testing hypotheses. The first kind of error (α) occurs if a null hypothesis (H_0) is true but was rejected. The probability of this kind of error is given by the chosen level of significance. An error of the second kind (β) occurs if a null hypothesis is false

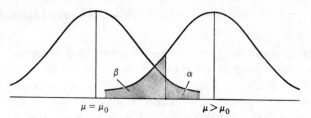

Figure 2-7 Type I error (α) and type II error (β) in hypothesis testing.

but is not rejected. Figure 2-7 shows the two types of error in hypothesis testing.

The third step in testing an hypothesis is to specify the level of significance in advance. The level of significance is used to decide whether to accept or reject the hypothesis. The approach is to hold the probability of the first kind of error constant and to minimize the probability of an error of the second kind. The concept of "statistically significant" refers to a significant difference between the hypothetical and estimated sample value. When H_0 is rejected, the results are statistically significant.

The most commonly used values for the level of significance range from 0.10 to 0.01. The choice of the level of significance is arbitrarily specified. The smaller the value of the level of significance that is chosen, the smaller the risk of rejecting a true null hypothesis. Once we have decided on the level of significance, the critical value is specified. The critical value is a value that specifies the location of a critical region within which we will reject a null hypothesis about a population parameter.

For example, when we test an hypothesis regarding the population mean μ of a normal population for a large sample, given the information σ^2, we compute Z according to Equation (2-15). The calculated Z is compared with the critical value. When the calculated Z is larger than the critical value, we reject the null hypothesis H_0.

2.4.2 Testing a Mean

The most simple and common example of hypothesis testing is a test of an hypothesis about a population mean.

Suppose, for example, that the average weight of college men is suspected to be 165 lb (μ). It is assumed that human weights are normally distributed with standard deviation of 5 lb (σ). Given the sample mean of 170 ($\overline{X}$), we want to test the hypothesis for the population mean. The hypothesis can be stated as follows:

$$H_0 : \mu = 165$$
$$H_a : \mu \neq 165.$$

We can apply the standardized normal Equation (2-15)

$$Z = \frac{\overline{X} - \mu}{\sigma}$$
$$= \frac{170 - 165}{5}.$$

Here the Z value is 1. Assume 0.05 as the level of significance; the critical value is 1.96 according to Table 1 of Appendix B. Since the calculated Z value is less than the critical value, we do not reject the null hypothesis.

When the population variance is unknown and the sample is small, say less than 30 observations, we have to rely on the t distribution, assuming that samples are from a normal distribution. We compute t according to Equation (2-24). The calculated t is compared with the critical value of the level of significance. When the former is larger than the latter, we reject the null hypothesis.

2.4.3 Two-Tailed Tests Versus One-Tailed Tests

In hypothesis testing, researchers often have the problem of choosing whether they should use two-tailed or one-tailed tests. This problem can be resolved if we review our setting of alternative hypothesis (H_a). For example, if we have

$$H_0 : \mu = \mu_0$$
$$H_a : \mu \neq \mu_0$$

then H_a implies that μ can be either larger or smaller than μ_0. On the other hand, if we have

$$H_0 : \mu = \mu_0$$
$$H_a : \mu > \mu_0 ,$$

or

$$H_0 : \mu = \mu_0$$
$$H_a : \mu < \mu_0 ,$$

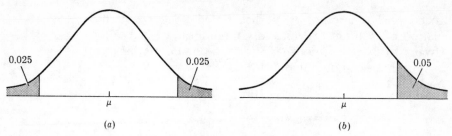

Figure 2-8   Regions of rejection in (a) two-tailed and (b) one-tailed tests.

then H_a implies that μ is larger than μ_0 in the former case, or H_a implies that μ is smaller than μ_0 in the latter case. This will imply that the researcher is certain about the alternative outcome of μ with respect to μ_0. Thus a one-tailed test is required.

Figure 2-8(a) illustrates the two-tailed test, and Figure 2-8(b) illustrates the one-tailed test. It is obvious that with the same amount of rejection region a one-tailed test has a larger chance to reject the null hypothesis than a two-tailed test. For instance, in the normal distribution the critical value that corresponds to the one-tailed area of 0.05 is 1.65, whereas the critical value that corresponds to the two-tailed area of 0.05 is 1.96.

2.4.4 Testing Difference of Two Means

A frequent problem in statistical inference is to test whether two samples are taken from the same distribution. Suppose that μ_1 and μ_2 be the means and σ_1^2 and σ_2^2 the variances for two populations, respectively. The hypotheses to be tested are

$$H_0 : \mu_1 - \mu_2 = 0$$
$$H_a : \mu_1 - \mu_2 \neq 0 .$$

Two separate samples are drawn at random which results in two sample means $\overline{X}_1$ and $\overline{X}_2$. The test of difference for two means is essentially to test if deviation between $\overline{X}_1$ and $\overline{X}_2$ is significantly different from 0.

In order to test this we must know the distribution of $\overline{X}_1$ and $\overline{X}_2$. We assume that X_1 and X_2 are independent of each other and are both normally distributed. The variances of $\overline{X}_1$ and $\overline{X}_2$ are σ^2/n_1 and σ^2/n_2, respectively.

The standardized normal equation then becomes

$$Z = \frac{(\overline{X}_1 - \overline{X}_2) - (\mu_1 - \mu_2)}{\sigma_m} = \frac{\overline{X}_1 - \overline{X}_2}{\sigma_m}$$

where

$$\sigma_m = \sqrt{\frac{\sigma_1^2}{n_1} + \frac{\sigma_2^2}{n_2}}. \qquad (2\text{-}29)$$

The comparison between the calculated Z value and the critical value of the level of significance decides the result of the hypothesis test.

When the population variances are not known, the t test can be applied in a form similar to Equation (2-29), such that

$$t = \frac{\overline{X}_1 - \overline{X}_2}{S_m} \qquad (2\text{-}30)$$

where

$$S_m = \sqrt{\frac{S_1^2}{n_1} + \frac{S_2^2}{n_2}}.$$

S_1^2 is the sample variance for X_1 with size n_1, and S_2^2 is the sample variance with size n_2. The t test in this case is with $n_1 + n_2 - 2$ degrees of freedom.

2.5   Analysis of Variance

Previous discussions on hypothesis testing are applied to test a sample mean against its population mean or to test the difference between two sample means. What if we were going to test the difference between two variances, or to test not just two sample means but three or more sample means? The answer is that the analysis-of-variance technique can be used for testing the hypothesis that three or more samples were drawn from the same normally distributed population. This test is performed by using the F distribution.

2.5.1   Inference about Difference between Two Variances: The F Distribution

If w_1 and w_2 are independent random variables having chi-square distribution with n_1 and n_2 degrees of freedom respectively, then

$$F = \frac{w_1/n_1}{w_2/n_2} \qquad (2\text{-}31)$$

has an F distribution with n_1 and n_2 degrees of freedom.

$p(x)$

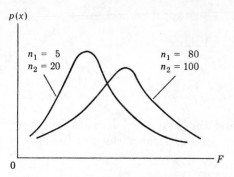

Figure 2-9 The F distribution with various degrees of freedom in numerator and denominator.

The F distribution is a unimodal curve skewed to the right, as shown in Figure 2-9. The parameters of the F distribution are the degrees of freedom of the numerator (n_1) and of the denominator n_2. Table 3 of Appendix B gives the calculated values for the F distribution.

One application of Equation (2-31) arises in problems in which we are interested in comparing the variances of two normal populations. For example, in testing $\sigma_1^2 = \sigma_2^2$, we can formulate two independent random variables according to Equation (2-27):

$$\frac{(n_1 - 1)\, s_1^2}{\sigma_1^2} \quad \text{and} \quad \frac{(n_2 - 1)\, s_2^2}{\sigma_2^2}.$$

These two variables have chi-square distributions with $n_1 - 1$ and $n_2 - 1$ degrees of freedom. Under the assumption that $\sigma_1^2 = \sigma_2^2$, we can construct an F ratio,

$$F = \frac{s_1^2}{s_2^2} \tag{2-32}$$

with $n_1 - 1$ and $n_2 - 1$ degrees of freedom. In this case our decision to accept the hypothesis of $\sigma_1^2 = \sigma_2^2$ is based on the value for the ratio of the two sample variances. Therefore, F is also called the variance ratio. If the F ratio is high, we tend not to accept the hypothesis.

In addition to testing the differences between two variances, the F distribution is widely used in the analysis of variance technique (discussed in the following sections).

2.5.2 One-Way Analysis of Variance

The general approach of the analysis of variance technique is to assume that there are independent random sam-

30

ples of size n from k populations and that X_{ij} is the jth observation from the ith sample.   Further, we assume that the corresponding random variables X_{ij} have independent normal distributions with means μ_i and common variance σ^2.   The general model can be stated as follows:

$$X_{ij} = \mu + \alpha_i + e_{ij} \quad \text{for } \begin{array}{l} i = 1, 2, \ldots, k \\ j = 1, 2, \ldots, n, \end{array} \quad (2\text{-}33)$$

where μ is the grand mean, α_i is the effect of the ith population, and e_{ij} is a random variable having normal distribution with 0 mean and the common variance σ^2.   Note that $\sum_{i=1}^{k} \alpha_i = 0$.   The null hypothesis of the test is that

$$\alpha_1 = \cdots = \alpha_k = 0.$$

To test the hypothesis we have to consider the total variability of the data.   Consider the sum of squared deviations of the X_{ij}'s in the k groups about the grand mean: $\sum_{i=1}^{k} \sum_{j=1}^{n} (X_{ij} - \overline{X})^2$, which may be decomposed into

$$\sum_{i=1}^{k} \sum_{j=1}^{n} (X_{ij} - \overline{X})^2 = \sum_{i=1}^{k} \sum_{j=1}^{n} [(X_{ij} - \overline{X}_i) + (\overline{X}_i - \overline{X})]^2$$

$$(2\text{-}34)$$

where

$$\overline{X} = \frac{1}{k \cdot n} \sum_{i=1}^{k} \sum_{j=1}^{n} X_{ij}$$

$$\overline{X}_i = \frac{1}{n} \sum_{j=1}^{n} X_{ij}.$$

If we expand the righthand term of Equation (2-34), we get

$$\sum_{i=1}^{k} \sum_{j=1}^{n} (X_{ij} - \overline{X})^2 = \sum_{i=1}^{k} \sum_{j=1}^{n} (X_{ij} - \overline{X}_i)^2$$

$$+ \sum_{i=1}^{k} \sum_{j=1}^{n} (\overline{X}_i - \overline{X})^2$$

$$+ 2 \sum_{i=1}^{k} \sum_{n=1}^{n} (X_{ij} - \overline{X}_i)(\overline{X}_i - \overline{X})$$

$$= \sum_{i=1}^{k} \sum_{j=1}^{n} (X_{ij} - \overline{X}_i)^2 + \sum_{i=1}^{} n_i (\overline{X}_i - \overline{X})^2,$$

$$(2\text{-}35)$$

since $\sum (X_{ij} - \overline{X}_i) = 0$.   Thus the total variation of X_{ij} (sum of squared deviations about the grand mean) is decomposed into the within-group variation (sum of squared deviations about the respective group means) plus the between-group variation (weighted sum of squared deviations of the group means about the grand mean).

To test a hypothesis about differences among the means of k groups is essentially to determine whether or not the differences among k-group means are greater than the variability resulting from random differences between elements within the groups. In other words, when the group means differ substantially from one another as compared with the variation of the observations within these groups, the null hypothesis that there is no difference among k-group means is not accepted.

A standard test of the null hypothesis that the mean classification is irrelevant ($\Sigma_{i=1}^{k} \alpha_i = 0$) might be based on the following ratio of the mean squared deviations:

$$F = \frac{\sum_{i=1}^{k} n_i (\overline{X}_i - \overline{X})^2 / k - 1}{\sum_{i=1}^{k} \sum_{j=1}^{n} (X_{ij} - \overline{X}_i)^2 / k(n-1)}. \qquad (2\text{-}36)$$

When the F ratio is large, this implies that the group means are substantially different from each other than the variations of the observations within these groups. Therefore, we reject the null hypothesis when the F ratio is large.

The following is an example for the application of the analysis of variance. Suppose that a car dealer, looking at the records of his five salesmen over the course of the year at three different time intervals, came up with the following data.

	Salesman			
1	2	3	4	5
23	17	31	38	26
57	33	35	34	16
37	49	16	35	31

This dealer would like to know whether or not the salesmen are equally good.

To test this, we set up a null hypothesis that

$$\alpha_1 = \alpha_2 = \alpha_3 = \alpha_4 = \alpha_5 = 0.$$

Based on the data presented, we have $k = 5$ and $n_1 = n_2 = n_3 = n_4 = n_5 = 3$. We can also calculate the sum of squared deviations about the respective means,

$$\sum_{i=1}^{k} \sum_{j=1}^{n} (X_{ij} - \bar{X}_i)^2 = 432.06 \, ,$$

and the weighted sum of squared deviations of the group means about the grand mean is

$$\sum_{i=1}^{k} n_i (X_i - \bar{\bar{X}})^2 = 1422.01 \, .$$

According to Equation (2.36), we can compute the F ratio as follows:

$$F = \frac{432.02/(5 - 1)}{1422.01/(15 - 5)} = 0.76 \, .$$

At the 5% level of significance, $F(4,10)$ is 3.48. Therefore, we do not reject the hypothesis that all salesmen are equally good. This example examines only the possible significant differences among the five salesmen as a whole. It does not examine the pairwise difference, such as whether salesman 1 is different from salesman 5. In an examination of the total sales between salesman 1 and salesman 5 it is not conceivable that they are indifferent. Therefore, students should be careful in using statistical tests. This example shows how formal statistical tests can be misleading.

So far we have discussed the case of one-way analysis of variance. One-way analysis of variance should help us to understand the more general technique in the analysis of variance such as two-way or three-way analysis of variance. However, the computations of the two-way and the three-way analyses of variance are much more complicated. Therefore, we will not present them here. These methods can be found in most statistics textbooks.

2.5.3 Limitations of Analysis of Variance

The parameters of the general model Equation (2-33), μ and α_i, can also be estimated by the least-squares method. The estimates of μ and α_i are the values that minimize

$$\sum_{i=1}^{k} \sum_{j=1}^{n} [X_{ij} - (\mu + \alpha_i)]^2 \qquad \text{(2-37)}$$

subject to the restriction that $\sum_{i=1}^{k} \alpha_i = 0$.

Review of Statistical Inference

From the point of view of testing the hypothesis, analysis of variance and regression are equivalent. If we are interested only in testing the hypothesis and if the classification is based on one or two criteria, the analysis of variance provides an efficient approach. For multiple criteria with equal numbers of observations in the categories the regression analysis is more efficient. If we are interested not only in testing hypotheses but also in estimating the parameters, we have to rely on the regression analysis. In a sense, analysis of variance is a special case of regression analysis. The rest of this text is devoted to the discussion of regression analysis.

3

SINGLE-EQUATION REGRESSION MODEL

3.1 Two-Variable Linear Model

The simplest economic relationship is a two-variable function. For example, quantity demanded is a function of price, production costs depend on rate of production, or consumption is a function of income. However, more realistic formulations require the specification of several variables in each function. To simplify the presentation of the estimation for these relationships statistically, we examine first the two-variable linear equation model, namely

$$Y = a + bX, \qquad (3\text{-}1)$$

where a and b are unknown parameters indicating the intercept and the slope of the function, respectively. They are also called the regression coefficients.

3.1.1 Random Disturbance

As we mentioned in the introduction chapter, relationships among economic variables are such that not every observation falls exactly on a line. Therefore, we must introduce a random disturbance or error term U into the equation:

$$Y = a + bX + U. \qquad (3\text{-}2)$$

There are several justifications for the introduction of an error term into the equation. First, we may commit a sampling error. For instance, consider Equation (3-2) as a household-consumption function, where Y is consumption and X is income. Even if Equation (3-2) is a correct relationship, the sample we randomly choose to examine may turn out to be predominantly poor families. Thus our estimates of a and b from this sample group may not be as good as the estimates obtained from a balanced sample group.

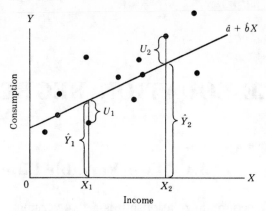

Figure 3-1 Least-squares fitting and random disturbances.

Second, we may have errors of specification. Theory represents a simplification of fact. It is not always possible to include all relevant variables in the functional relation. For example, in a consumption function, consumer tastes, his wealth, and market interest rates are sometimes omitted in a household-consumption function. Some of these omitted variables have positive effects on consumption, while others have negative effects on consumption. Some of these omitted variables are quantifiable while others are not. The net effects of these omitted variables in the equation are represented by the error term.†

Third, the data we obtained may have errors of measurement. It is likely that income and consumption information we obtained from a household may not be accurate. If the data are obtained from a government statistical report, the data may not be accurate as a result of clerical handling and rounding error.

When Equation (3-2) has either one or more of these three sources of error, it is justified for the introduction of an error term. Figure 3-1 illustrates Equation (3-2) using a household consumption as an example.

3.1.2 Statistical Assumptions in Linear Model

In order to estimate the parameters of the model statistically, the relationship in Equation (3-2) requires

---

†Readers may wonder why Equation (3-2) has a constant term a. One way to justify this is to consider $Y = bX + V$, where V is a residual with no guarantee that V has a mean of 0. Define $U = V - a$ and let $U = 0$ so that $Y = a + bX + U$.

some assumptions about the probability distribution of the error term.

1. The simplest assumption is that the expected value of the error term is 0; that is

$$E(U_i) = 0 \quad \text{for } i = 1, 2, \ldots, n. \tag{3-3}$$

   where i is the ith sample observation of size n.

2. The variance of the error term is assumed to be constant; that is

$$V(U_i) = E(U_i - EU)^2 = E(U_i)^2 = \sigma^2$$
$$\text{for } i = 1, 2, \ldots, n. \tag{3-4}$$

3. We assume that the various values of the error term are uncorrelated to each other; that is

$$E(U_i U_j) = 0 \quad \text{for } i \neq j, i, j = 1, 2, \ldots, n. \tag{3-5}$$

4. Finally, we assume explanatory variable X's are constants that can be obtained in repeated sample. Therefore the X's are uncorrelated to the error term. This assumption implies

$$E(X_i U_i) = 0 \quad \text{for } i = 1, 2, \ldots, n. \tag{3-6}$$

The assumptions above stated are developed in the classical linear regression model. The proof of the properties of least-squares estimators, shown in Section 3.3, is based upon these four assumptions.

In Chapter 1, we discussed the fact that economic data are not obtained under experimental control; thus, the assumption that the explanatory variable X's are constants is a very rigid requirement. However, one can relax this rigid assumption by assuming that X's are independent random variables and also that the conditional distributions of the Y's, given X, are independent with expectations, given $E(Y_i|X_i) = a + bX_i$ and with constant variance of the error term. This modified assumption enables us to apply statistical inference when the X's are not constant.

3.2   Least-Squares Estimator

Given a set of n observations on two variables Y and X,

$$(Y_1, Y_2, \ldots, Y_n)$$
$$(X_1, X_2, \ldots, X_n),$$

Single-Equation Regression Model

we want to estimate the relationship between Y and X from the sample observations above such that

$$\hat{Y} = \hat{a} + \hat{b}X, \tag{3-7}$$

where $\hat{a}$ and $\hat{b}$ are estimates of the unknown parameters a and b and where $\hat{Y}$ is the estimated value of Y. The deviations between the observed and estimated values of Y are called residuals e,

$$e = Y - \hat{Y}. \tag{3-8}$$

The principle of least squares is to choose the $\hat{a}$, $\hat{b}$ values that will minimize the sum of squared deviations between the observed and estimated values of Y, $\sum_{i=1}^{n} e_i^2$.

Therefore, the estimated equation will be the best-fitting curve on the least-squares criterion.

According to Equation (3-8),

$$\sum_{i=1}^{n} e_i^2 = \sum_{i=1}^{n} (Y_i - \hat{Y}_i)^2 \quad \text{where } i = 1, 2, \ldots, n$$

$$= \sum_{i=1}^{n} (Y_i - \hat{a} - \hat{b}X_i)^2 .$$

A necessary condition to minimize $\sum_{i=1}^{n} e_i^2$ is that

$$\frac{\partial}{\partial \hat{a}} \sum_{i=1}^{n} e_i^2 = -2 \sum_{i=1}^{n} (Y_i - \hat{a} - \hat{b}X_i) = 0$$

$$\frac{\partial}{\partial \hat{b}} \sum_{i=1}^{n} e_i^2 = -2 \sum_{i=1}^{n} X_i(Y_i - \hat{a} - \hat{b}X_i) = 0.$$

Rearranging these two equations gives the "normal equations":

$$\sum_{i=1}^{n} Y_i = n\hat{a} + \hat{b} \sum_{i=1}^{n} X_i \tag{3-9}$$

and

$$\sum_{i=1}^{n} X_i Y_i = \hat{a} \sum_{i=1}^{n} X_i + \hat{b} \sum_{i=1}^{n} X_i^2 . \tag{3-10}$$

Given the observed values of Y_i and X_i, $\hat{a}$ and $\hat{b}$ can be solved from simultaneous Equations (3-9) and (3-10).

$$b = \frac{\left(\sum\limits_{i=1}^{n} X_i\right)\left(\sum\limits_{i=1}^{n} Y_i\right) - n \sum\limits_{i=1}^{n} X_i Y_i}{\left(\sum\limits_{i=1}^{n} X_i\right)^2 - n \sum\limits_{i=1}^{n} X_i^2} \qquad (3\text{-}11)$$

and

$$\hat{a} = \overline{Y} - \hat{b}\overline{X}, \qquad (3\text{-}12)$$

where

$$\overline{Y} = \frac{1}{n} \sum\limits_{i=1}^{n} Y_i \quad \text{and} \quad \overline{X} = \frac{1}{n} \sum\limits_{i=1}^{n} X_i.$$

An alternative approach to solve for $\hat{a}$ and $\hat{b}$ is by the deviations from the means of X and Y, that is,

$$x_i = X_i - \overline{X} \qquad y_i = Y_i - \overline{Y} \qquad \hat{y}_i = \hat{Y}_i - \overline{\hat{Y}} = \hat{Y}_i - \overline{Y}.$$

Equation (3-12) shows that the fitted line passes through the mean point $(\overline{Y},\overline{X})$. Its equation can, therefore, be written:

$$(Y - \overline{Y}) = \hat{b}(X - \overline{X}). \qquad (3\text{-}13)$$

Substituting Equation (3-12) into Equation (3-10) and rearranging Equation (3-10) gives the following expression:

$$\hat{b} = \frac{\sum\limits_{i=1}^{n} X_i Y_i - n\overline{X}\overline{Y}}{\sum\limits_{i=1}^{n} X_i^2 - n\overline{X}^2}$$

$$= \frac{\sum\limits_{i=1}^{n} x_i y_i}{\sum\limits_{i=1}^{n} x_i^2}. \qquad (3\text{-}14)$$

Notice the solutions for $\hat{b}$ expressed by either Equation (3-11) or Equation (3-14) are algebraically equivalent. Students should be able to verify that this is the case.

There are a number of algebraic properties about $\sum_{i=1}^{n} Y_i$, $\sum_{i=1}^{n} \hat{Y}_i$, and $\sum_{i=1}^{n} e_i$:

1. The sum of the estimated Y's equals the sum of the observed Y's.

$$\sum_{i=1}^{n} \hat{Y}_i = \sum_{i=1}^{n} (\hat{a} + \hat{b}X_i) \qquad \text{by Equation (3-7)}$$

$$= n\hat{a} + \hat{b} \sum_{i=1}^{n} X_i$$

$$= \sum_{i=1}^{n} Y_i \qquad \text{by Equation (3-9)} \qquad (3\text{-}15)$$

2. The sum of residuals is 0:

$$\sum_{i=1}^{n} e_i = \sum_{i=1}^{n} (Y_i - \hat{Y}_i) \qquad \text{by Equation (3-15). } (3\text{-}16)$$

3. The sum of the cross products of the explanatory variable X and the residuals is 0:

$$\sum_{i=1}^{n} X_i e_i = \sum_{i=1}^{n} X_i(Y_i - \hat{Y}_i)$$

$$= \sum_{i=1}^{n} XY - \sum_{i=1}^{n} X_i(\hat{a} + \hat{b}X_i) \qquad \text{by Equation (3-10)}$$

$$= 0. \qquad (3\text{-}17)$$

4. The sum of the cross products of the estimated value Y and the residuals is also 0.

$$\sum_{i=1}^{n} \hat{Y}_i e_i = \sum_{i=1}^{n} (\hat{a} + \hat{b}X_i) e_i$$

$$= \hat{a} \sum_{i=1}^{n} e_i + \hat{b} \sum_{i=1}^{n} X_i e_i$$

$$= 0 + \hat{b} \cdot 0 \qquad \text{by Equations (3-16) and (3-17)}$$

$$= 0. \qquad (3\text{-}18)$$

5. The sum of squared observed Y's equals the sum of squared estimated Y's plus the sum of squared residuals.

$$\sum_{i=1}^{n} Y_i^2 = \sum_{i=1}^{n} (\hat{Y}_i + e_i)^2 \qquad \text{by Equation (3-8)}$$

$$= \sum_{i=1}^{n} \hat{Y}_i^2 + \sum_{i=1}^{n} e_i^2 + 2 \sum_{i=1}^{n} \hat{Y}e_i$$

$$= \sum_{i=1}^{n} \hat{Y}_i^2 + \sum_{i=1}^{n} e_i^2 \qquad \text{by Equation (3-18).}$$

$$(3\text{-}19)$$

It is also true that from Equation (3-19)

$$\sum_{i=1}^{n} y_i^2 = \sum_{i=1}^{n} \hat{y}_i^2 + \sum_{i=1}^{n} e_i^2. \qquad (3\text{-}20)$$

The results of Equations (3-19) and (3-20) imply that the total sum of squares (SST) equals the regression sum of squares (SSR) plus the error sum of squares (SSE). The meaning of Equation (3-20) is similar to Equation (2-15) of the analysis of variance. As we shall show below, Equation (3-19) or Equation (3-20) is the basis of the analysis of variance for the two-variable case.

Following is a numerical illustration of estimating a least-squares equation.

Y	X	$y = Y - \overline{Y}$	$x = X - \overline{X}$
40	4	-22	-4
60	6	-2	-2
50	7	-12	-1
70	10	8	2
90	13	28	5

The information above gives us

$$n = 5 \qquad \sum Y = 310 \qquad \sum X = 40$$

$$\sum XY = 2740 \qquad \sum X^2 = 370$$

$$\sum xy = 260 \qquad \sum x^2 = 50.$$

From Equations (3-11) and (3-12)

$$\hat{b} = \frac{(40)(310) - 5(2740)}{(40)^2 - 5(370)} = 5.2$$

$$\hat{a} = 62 - 41.6 = 20.4,$$

and the estimated relation is written

$$\hat{Y} = 20.4 + 5.2X.$$

Using deviations from the means and using Equations (3-12) and (3-14) we obtain, as before,

$$\hat{b} = \frac{260}{50} = 5.2 \qquad \hat{a} = 20.4.$$

41

The five algebraic properties can also be confirmed.

1. $\Sigma \hat{Y} = 41.2 + 51.6 + 56.8 + 72.4 + 88.0 = 310$
$\Sigma Y = 40 + 60 + 50 + 70 + 90 = 310$

2. $\Sigma e = \Sigma(Y - \hat{Y}) = -1.2 + 8.4 - 6.8 - 2.4 + 2.0 = 0$

3. $\Sigma Xe = -4.8 + 50.4 - 47.6 - 24.0 + 26.0 = 0$

4. $\Sigma \hat{Y}e = -49.44 + 433.44 - 386.24 - 173.76$
$+ 176.00 = 0$

5. $\Sigma Y^2 = \Sigma \hat{Y}^2 + \Sigma e^2 = 20{,}572 + 128 = 20{,}700$
$\Sigma Y^2 = 1600 + 3600 + 25{,}000 + 4900 + 8100$
$= 20{,}700$ or
$\Sigma y^2 = \Sigma \hat{y}^2 + \Sigma e_2 = 1352 + 128 = 1480$
$\Sigma y^2 = 484 + 4 + 144 + 64 + 784 = 1480.$

3.3 Properties of Least-Squares Estimators

We have stated four statistical assumptions, Equations (3-3) through (3-6), about the linear-regression model in Section 3.1. We repeat these assumptions here again:

$$E(U_i) = 0 \qquad i = 1, 2, \ldots, n \qquad (3\text{-}3)$$

$$V(U_i) = \sigma^2 \qquad\qquad\qquad (3\text{-}4)$$

$$E(U_i U_j) = 0 \qquad i \ne j; i, j = 1, 2, \ldots, n \qquad (3\text{-}5)$$

$$E(X_i U_i) = 0. \qquad\qquad\qquad (3\text{-}6)$$

These four assumptions imply that error terms U has 0 mean and common variance σ^2 and that error terms are uncorrelated to each other. Furthermore, X_i and U_i are also uncorrelated.

Based on these assumptions we will develop the statistical properties of the estimators, $\hat{a}$ and $\hat{b}$. The properties of $\hat{a}$ and $\hat{b}$ are exactly the same. To avoid repetition, we discuss $\hat{b}$ only.† First, $\hat{b}$ is an unbiased linear estimator of b. (The concept of unbiasedness was discussed in Section 2.3.1.)

From Equation (3-14) we can write:‡

---

†For $\hat{a}$, see Johnston, *Econometric Methods* (New York, McGraw-Hill, 1963), pp. 14-20.

‡From now on it is understood that $\Sigma_{i=1}^{n}$ is simplified as Σ.

3.3 Properties of Least-Squares Estimators

$$\hat{b} = \frac{\sum x_i y_i}{\sum x_i^2} = \frac{\sum x_i Y_i}{\sum x_i^2} - \frac{\overline{Y}\sum x_i}{\sum x_i^2} \qquad \text{since } y_i = Y_i - \overline{Y}$$

$$= \frac{\sum x_i Y_i}{\sum x_i^2} \qquad \text{since } \sum x_i = 0$$

$$= \frac{\sum x_i}{\sum x_i^2}(a + bX_i + U_i) \qquad \text{by Equation (3-2)}$$

$$= b\frac{\sum x_i X_i}{\sum x_i^2} + \frac{\sum x_i U_i}{\sum x_i^2} \qquad \text{since } \sum x_i = 0.$$

Thus

$$\hat{b} = b + \frac{\sum x_i U_i}{\sum x_i^2} \qquad\qquad (3\text{-}21)$$

since

$$\frac{\sum x_i X_i}{\sum x_i^2} = \frac{\sum x_i (x_i + \overline{X})}{\sum x_i^2} = 1.$$

Take the expected value of Equation (3-21):

$$E(\hat{b}) = b + \frac{E\left(\sum x_i U_i\right)}{\sum x_i^2} = b \qquad \text{using Equation (3-6).}$$

Hence $\hat{b}$ is an unbiased estimate of b. The assumption of constant X values in the algebraic operations above implied that $\hat{b}$ is a linear function of b. Thus $\hat{b}$ is an unbiased linear estimator of b.

Next we establish that the variance of $\hat{b}$ is the best among a class of linear unbiased estimators; that is, $\hat{b}$ has the smallest variance. Let us obtain the variance of $\hat{b}$, $\sigma_{\hat{b}}^2$, or $V(\hat{b})$, first; namely,

$$\sigma_{\hat{b}}^2 = E(\hat{b} - b)^2 = E\left(\frac{\sum x_i U_i}{\sum x_i^2}\right)^2 \qquad \text{by Equation (3-20)}$$

$$= E\left[\frac{1}{(\sum x_i^2)^2}(x_1^2 U_1^2 + x_2^2 U_2^2 + \cdots + x_n^2 U_n^2\right.$$

$$\left. + 2x_1 x_2 U_1 U_2 + \cdots + 2x_{n-1} x_n U_{n-1} U_n)\right]$$

$$= \frac{\sum x_i^2}{(\sum x_i^2)^2}\sigma^2 \qquad \text{by Equations (3-4), (3-5), and (3-6).}$$

Thus

$$\sigma_{\hat{b}}^2 = \frac{\sigma^2}{\sum x_i^2} . \tag{3-22}$$

To prove that $\hat{b}$ has the smallest variance of all linear unbiased estimates, we define

$$\hat{\hat{b}} = \sum c_i Y_i,$$

where

$$c_i = \frac{x_i}{\sum x_i^2} + d_i, \tag{3-23}$$

and where d_i are arbitrary constants. $\hat{\hat{b}}$ can be rewritten as

$$\hat{\hat{b}} = \sum c_i (a + bX_i + U_i).$$

Therefore

$$E(\hat{\hat{b}}) = a \sum c_i + b \sum c_i X_i.$$

To show $E(\hat{\hat{b}}) = b$, we must assume that $\sum c_i = 0$ and that $\sum c_i X_i = 1$. These two conditions require, according to Equation (3-23), that

$$\sum d_i = 0 \quad \text{and} \quad \sum d_i X_i = \sum d_i x_i = 0.$$

The variance of $\hat{\hat{b}}$ is then

$$\sigma_{\hat{\hat{b}}}^2 = E(\hat{\hat{b}} - b)^2$$

$$= E \left(\sum c_i U_i \right)^2$$

$$= \sigma^2 \sum c_i^2 \quad \text{by Equations (3-4) and (3-5)}$$

$$= \sigma^2 \left[\sum \left(\frac{x_i}{\sum x_i^2} \right)^2 + \sum d_i^2 + 2 \sum \frac{x_i}{x_i^2} d_i \right]$$

$$= \frac{\sigma^2}{\sum x_i^2} + \sigma_2 \sum d_i^2$$

$$= \sigma_{\hat{b}}^2 + \sigma^2 \sum d_i^2 .$$

Therefore, $\sigma_{\hat{\hat{b}}}^2$ is at least equal to or larger than $\sigma_{\hat{b}}^2$, since $\sum d_i^2$ is at least 0 or larger. This result demonstrates that, in fact, $\hat{b}$ has the smallest variance of all linear unbiased estimates. We conclude that $\hat{b}$ is a best unbiased linear estimate.

3.4   Statistical Inference in Regression Model

3.4.1   Estimation of Standard Error of Estimate and Standard Error of Coefficient

To make statistical inferences about $\hat{b}$ or to test its statistical significance, we have to know the variance of $\hat{b}$. According to Equation (3-21), the variance of $\hat{b}$ is a function of the disturbance variance σ^2. Therefore, an estimator of the disturbance variance σ^2 should first be obtained from the sample observations in order to estimate the variance of $\hat{b}$.

The estimation of σ^2 can be based on the error sum of squares Σe^2 :

$$e_i = Y_i - \hat{Y}_i$$
$$= (y_i + \overline{Y}) - (\hat{y}_i + \overline{Y}) \quad \text{since } \hat{y}_i = \hat{Y}_i - \overline{\hat{Y}} = \hat{Y} - \overline{Y}$$
$$= y_i - \hat{y}_i.$$

Averaging $Y_i = a + bX_i + U_i$ over the n sample observations, we obtain $\overline{Y} = a + b\overline{X} + \overline{U}$, so that

$$y_i = bx_i + (U_i - \overline{U}).$$

From the normal Equation (3-9),

$$\overline{Y} = \hat{a} + \hat{b}\overline{X}. \tag{3-24}$$

Subtracting Equation (3-24) from (3-7), we obtain

$$\hat{Y} - \overline{Y} = \hat{b}(X - \overline{X})$$

or

$$\hat{y}_i = \hat{b}x_i,$$

so that we have

$$e_i = -(\hat{b} - b)x_i + (U_i - \overline{U}).$$

Hence

$$\sum e_i^2 = (\hat{b} - b)^2 \sum x_i^2$$
$$+ \sum (U_i - \overline{U})^2 - 2(\hat{b} - b)\sum x_i(U_i - \overline{U}).$$

Taking the expected value of this equation we have

45

$$E\left(\sum e_i^2\right) = E\left\{(b - b)^2 \sum x_i^2 + \left[\sum U_i^2 - \frac{(\sum U_i)^2}{n}\right]\right.$$

$$\left. - 2\frac{\sum x_i U_i}{\sum x_i^2}\left(\sum x_i U_i - \sum x_i \overline{U}\right)\right\}$$

$$= \sigma^2 + (n - 1)\sigma^2 - 2E\left[\frac{(\sum x_i U_i)^2}{\sum x_i^2}\right]$$

$$\text{since } \sum x_i = 0$$

$$= \sigma^2 + (n - 1)\sigma^2 - 2\sigma^2 \qquad \text{using Equation (3-4)}$$

$$= (n - 2)\sigma^2.$$

Therefore,
$$S^2 = \frac{\sum e_i^2}{n - 2}, \tag{3-25}$$

where S^2 is an unbiased estimate of σ^2. S is a square root of S^2, and it is called the standard error of the estimate.

An unbiased estimate of $\sigma_{\hat{b}}^2$, $S_{\hat{b}}^2$, is obtainable by using Equation (3-21), so that

$$S_{\hat{b}}^2 = \frac{S^2}{\sum x_i^2} = \frac{\sum e_i^2}{(n - 2)\sum x_i^2} \tag{3-26}$$

The square root of $S_{\hat{b}}$, $S_{\hat{b}}^2$, is called the standard error of the coefficient.

Using the numerical example in Section 3.2, we can now illustrate the estimation of S^2 and S_b^2:

$$S^2 = \frac{128}{5 - 2} = 42.7$$

$$S_b^2 = \frac{42.7}{50} = 0.85.$$

3.4.2 Interval Estimation and Significance Tests

So far we have not specified the form of the distribution of the error term. In most cases we assume that the error term has the normal distribution. If we assume that U_i has a normal distribution, the maximum likelihood estimator of b and the least-squares estimator of b are equivalent.[†]

46

†Johnston, *op. cit.*, pp. 20-21.

3.4   Statistical Inference in Regression Model

From Equation (3-21) we see that $\hat{b}$ is a linear function of U_i. Therefore, if we assume that the U_i are normally distributed, $\hat{b}$ is also normally distributed. Since $E\hat{b} = b$ and $\sigma_{\hat{b}}^2 = \dfrac{\sigma^2}{\Sigma x_i^2}$, then

$$\frac{\hat{b} - b}{\sigma_{\hat{b}}} \qquad\qquad (3\text{-}27)$$

is distributed normally with 0 mean and unit variance, where $\sigma_{\hat{b}}$ is the standard error of the b. However, when σ^2 and x_b^2 are unknown, we have to make use of our knowledge of S^2 and $S_{\hat{b}}^2$ so that

$$\frac{\hat{b} - b}{S_{\hat{b}}} \qquad\qquad (3\text{-}28)$$

has t distribution with $n - 2$ degrees of freedom. Equation (3-28) permits us to construct a confidence interval for b or to test the hypothesis that $\hat{b} = b$.

The estimation of confidence interval for b, say at a 95% level, indicates that in repeated samples there would be a tendency to include the true value of b in the interval 95% of the time. The choice of a 95% level of confidence is arbitrary but fairly conventional. One stronger choice would be a 99% level of confidence, while a weaker choice would be a 90% level of confidence. For smaller levels of confidence the t value will be smaller, and for higher levels the t value will be higher.

The formula for the estimation of the confidence interval for b is

$$\hat{b} + t_{\frac{\alpha}{2}} S_{\hat{b}} \; . \qquad\qquad (3\text{-}29)$$

From the numerical example in this chapter we know that $S_{\hat{b}} = 0.92$ and that $\hat{b} = 5.2$. From the t distribution table with $5 - 2$ degrees of freedom at a 95% of confidence interval, $t = 3.182$. Therefore, the estimated confidence interval at a 95% level is $5.2 \pm 3.182(0.92)$. In other words, in repeated sample experiments a 95% confidence interval covers the true value of b, which is 2.3 to 8.1.

The common approach in testing regression coefficients is to assume that $b = 0$. This assumption implies that a variable with a 0 coefficient in an equation carries

47

no weight in explaining the variation of the dependent variable; therefore, it may as well have been omitted. The approach in testing regression coefficients is to set

$$t = \frac{\hat{b}}{S_{\hat{b}}} ,$$

(3-30)

with the null hypothesis that $b = 0$. Equation (3-30) is referred to as the "t-ratio." A high t-ratio tends to reject the hypothesis that $b = 0$. This test need not be confined to $b = 0$. In many economic problems we are interested in parameters other than 0, such as unity.

The value of the t-ratio is negatively influenced by S_b. According to Equation (3-26), the standard error of the coefficient b varies inversely with the variation of x and the size of the sample. Therefore, it would be desirable to choose a large sample with wide variation that will give a reliable estimate of b. On the other hand, the standard error of b is positively related with the estimated variance of the error term. Therefore, a small variance-of-error term tends to give a high value of the t-ratio.

The numerical example has shown that $S_{\hat{b}} = 0.92$ and $\hat{b} = 5.2$. Thus, the calculated value of the t-ratio is 5.65. We choose a 5% level of significance (95% level of confidence), the value of t is 3.182 for a two-tail test with adjusted degrees of freedom, $5 - 2 = 3$. The calculated t value is higher than 3.182. Therefore, we reject the null hypothesis and conclude that X is a statistically significant variable in explaining the variation of Y.

3.4.3 Predictions

One of the objectives of econometrics is the prediction of economic phenomena. That is, given an X value, X_0, we want to predict the Y value. In other words,

$$Y_0 = a + bX_0 + U_0,$$

(3-31)

where U_0 is the disturbance. Again we assume that

$$E(U_0) = 0$$

and

$$E(U_0^2) = \sigma^2 .$$

If we predict Y_0 by

$$\hat{Y}_0 = \hat{a} + \hat{b}X_0,$$

48

the prediction error will be

$$\epsilon = Y_0 - \hat{Y}_0$$
$$= (a + bX_0 + U_0) - (\hat{a} + \hat{b}X_0).$$

The expectation of the prediction error will be

$$E\epsilon = E(a - \hat{a}) + E(b - \hat{b}) X_0 + E(U_0)$$
$$= 0 \quad \text{since } E(\hat{a}) = a, E(\hat{b}) = b.$$

Therefore, the predicted value of Y by Equation (3-31) is an unbiased estimate. In fact, it can be shown that $\hat{Y}_0$ is the best linear unbiased estimate.

It follows that the variance-of-prediction error will be

$$E(\epsilon - E\epsilon)^2 = E[(a - \hat{a}) + (b - \hat{b}) X_0 + U_0]^2$$
$$= E[(a - \hat{a}) + (b - \hat{b}) X_0]^2 + E(U_0)^2$$
$$= \sigma_{\hat{y}_0}^2 + \sigma^2, \tag{3-32}$$

where $\sigma_{\hat{y}_0}^2$ is $E[(a - \hat{a}) + (b - \hat{b}) X_0]^2$. Equation (3-32) implies that the error made in predicting an individual value is the sum of two uncorrelated errors: the error in estimating the parameters of the regression equation and the error of the random disturbance during the forecasting period.

Since prediction involves uncertainty, we will obtain the interval estimate of Y_0 based on the regression equation. This interval can be expressed as

$$Y_0 \pm t_{\frac{\alpha}{2}} \sqrt{\sigma_{\hat{y}_0}^2 + \sigma^2}. \tag{3-33}$$

3.4.4   Correlation Coefficient and Coefficient of Determination

The correlation coefficient is a measure of the degree of association between two variables. The crude measure of association between X_i and Y_i $(i = 1, 2, \ldots, n)$ is indicated by $\sum_{i=1}^{n} x_i y_i$. Figure 3-2 shows that for all points in quadrants I and III, $\sum x_i y_i$ is positive, which implies that X_i and Y_i have a positive relation, while for all points in quadrants II and IV, $\sum x_i y_i$ is negative, which implies that X_i and Y_i have a negative relation. However, this crude measurement cannot express the magnitude of association between two variables. The cross-product $\sum x_i y_i$ can be influenced by the units of measurement for X and Y. To standardize the measurement of association, each of the variables is divided by its standard deviation and averaged.

49

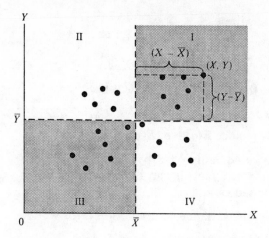

Figure 3-2 Scatter diagrams for X and Y and their association.

As such it becomes

$$\gamma = \frac{\sum x_i y_i}{n\, S_x S_y}, \tag{3-34}$$

where

$$S_x = \sqrt{\frac{\sum x_i^2}{n}} \quad \text{and} \quad S_y = \sqrt{\frac{\sum y_i^2}{n}}.$$

Equation (3-34) can be expressed as

$$\gamma = \frac{\sum x_i y_i}{\sqrt{\sum x_i^2}\ \sqrt{\sum y_i^2}}$$

$$= \frac{n\sum XY - (\sum X)(\sum Y)}{\sqrt{n\sum X^2 - (\sum X)^2}\ \sqrt{n\sum Y^2 - (\sum Y)^2}}. \tag{3-35}$$

From Equation (3-14)

$$\hat{b} = \frac{\sum x_i y_i}{\sum x_i^2}.$$

Substituting Equation (3-35) into Equation (3-14) we get

$$\hat{b} = \gamma \frac{S_Y}{S_X} \tag{3-36}$$

or

$$\gamma = \hat{b}\, \frac{S_X}{S_Y}. \tag{3-37}$$

3.4 Statistical Inference in Regression Model

Taking the square of Equation (3-37), we obtain

$$\gamma^2 = \frac{\hat{b}^2 \, S_X^2}{S_Y^2} = \frac{\hat{b}^2 \sum x_i^2}{\sum y_i^2}$$

$$= \frac{\sum \hat{y}_i^2}{\sum y_i^2} = \frac{SSR}{SST}, \qquad (3\text{-}38)$$

where γ^2 sometimes is called the coefficient of determination, $\sum y_i^2$ is the total variation of the Y values, and $\sum \hat{y}_i^2$ is the variation of Y explained by variations in X. Therefore, this coefficient indicates the proportion of the Y variance explained by the variation of X. Using Equation (3-38), we may write

$$\gamma^2 = 1 - \frac{SSE}{SST} = 1 - \frac{\sum e_i^2}{\sum y_i^2}. \qquad (3\text{-}39)$$

Since $\sum e_i^2$ has a limit between $\sum y_i^2$ and 0, γ^2 will lie between 0 and 1. When γ^2 is 0.95, it implies that the 95% of the variation of Y can be explained by the variation of X.

In most cases we use the notation R^2 as the coefficient of determination instead of γ^2. There is a slight difference between γ^2 and R^2. γ^2 denotes the coefficient of determination between two variables, while R^2 denotes the coefficient of determination of more than two-variable cases. Therefore, γ^2 is called the simple coefficient of determination, while R^2 is called multiple coefficient of determination. For simplicity, we will call R^2 the coefficient of determination regardless of the number of variables contained in the equation.

To test the significance of R^2 that R^2 is not different from 0, that Y is not explained by the explanatory variable in the equation, we can make use of F test. This is an example of the analysis of variance. In the case of two-variable models with the null hypothesis $b = 0$,

$$F = \frac{\hat{b}^2 \sum x_i^2 / (2-1)}{\sum e^2 / (n-2)} = \frac{\sum \hat{y}_i^2 / (2-1)}{\sum e^2 / (n-2)}$$

$$= \frac{SSR / (2-1)}{SSE / (n-2)}, \qquad (3\text{-}40)$$

where F has $(1, n-2)$ degrees of freedom. The high values of F leads to the rejection of the null hypothesis. Therefore, it is quite natural that rejection of the null hypothesis occurs when SSR is high relative to SSE; that is, when R^2 is high.

The F test is designed to test the significance of all variables or a set of variables in the equation. However, in the two-variable case the F test is used for testing the single explanatory variable and at the same time is equivalent to test the significance of R^2.

Following is a numerical example based on the information in Section 3.1:

$$n = 5 \qquad \sum x_i y_i = 260 \qquad \sum x_i^2 = 50$$

$$\sum y_i^2 = 1480 \qquad \sum \hat{y}_i^2 = 1352 \qquad \sum e_i^2 = 128$$

$$\gamma = \frac{260}{50 \cdot 1480} = 0.97$$

$$R^2 = \frac{1352}{1480} = 0.93.$$

The F value is calculated based on the information above as

$$F = \frac{1352/(2 - 1)}{128/(5 - 2)} = 31.68.$$

At a 5% level of significance $F(1,3)$ is 10.13, which is less that 31.68. Therefore, R^2 is statistically significant.

3.4.5 Correlation and Regression

The preceding section has shown that there is a close relation between correlation analysis and regression analysis. In fact, based on the results of regression analysis we can obtain the correlation coefficient between two variables.

The question then is under what conditions an application of regression analysis is more proper than the application of correlation analysis. In other words, are there any differences between these two methods? Several points can be made.

First, although both correlation and regression measure the association between two variables, correlation is a measure of a linear relation only; it is of no use in describing nonlinear relations. On the other hand, regression analysis can be performed depending on a specific functional form that can be either linear or nonlinear.

Second, recall that in the assumptions in the regression model, Section 3.1.2, the X variable can be either fixed or random. But the assumption in correlation analysis requires that both X and Y are random variables and have a bivariate normal distribution. Therefore, the application of regression analysis is broader than correlation analysis.

Third, correlation analysis measures only the degree of association between two variables. Although both correlation analysis and regression analysis cannot claim the cause and effect between these two variables, regression analysis can set up a hypothesis to confirm that variable X has an influence on variable Y. This test is equivalent to the t test of the significance of the regression coefficient.

Finally, the advantage of regression over correlation is that the regression method gives numerical estimates that are suitable for use in predicting future values of the dependent variable with knowledge of the independent variable.

The discussions above help us to understand why most of empirical researches in economics have relied heavily on regression analysis rather than on correlation analysis, although correlation is a useful aid to understand regression results.

3.5   Multiple-Regression Model

3.5.1 Estimation of Three-Variable Model

Usually when a regression equation has three or more than three variables, we call it a multiple-regression model. The statistical formulas for estimating parameters, variance, and testing the parameters are very similar, or in some cases identical, to the two-variable regression model.

The simplest example of a multiple-regression model is a three-variable case. If the reader can understand the analysis of a relationship between three variables, he should be able to generalize the concept of a multiple-regression model. A conventional example of a three-variable equation is a demand equation in which quantity demanded depends not only on the price of the commodity but also on the income of a consumer.

A three-variable regression model is written as follows:

$$Y_i = a + bX_{1i} + cX_{2i} + U_i \qquad i = 1, 2, \ldots, n, \qquad (3\text{-}41)$$

with the same assumptions about U_i and X_1 as those stated in Section 3.2.

Again, the relationships of X_1 and X_2 on Y are not exact; thus we write

$$Y_i = \hat{Y} + e_i$$
$$= \hat{a} + \hat{b}X_{1i} + \hat{c}X_{2i} + e_i. \qquad (3\text{-}42)$$

The least-squares estimators can be obtained by minimizing the sum of squared e_i. Then

$$\sum e_i^2 = \sum (Y_i - \hat{a} - \hat{b}X_{1i} - \hat{c}X_{2i})^2.$$

The partial derivatives with respect to $\hat{a}$, $\hat{b}$, and $\hat{c}$ are

$$\frac{\partial}{\partial \hat{a}} \sum e_i^2 = -2 \sum (Y_i - \hat{a} - \hat{b}X_{1i} - \hat{c}X_{2i})$$

$$\frac{\partial}{\partial \hat{b}} \sum e_i^2 = -2 \sum X_{1i}(Y_i - \hat{a} - \hat{b}X_{1i} - \hat{c}X_{2i})$$

and

$$\frac{\partial}{\partial \hat{c}} \sum e_i^2 = -2 \sum X_{2i}(Y_i - \hat{a} - \hat{b}X_{1i} - \hat{c}X_{2i}).$$

Equating these to 0 and rearranging, we obtain the following normal equations

$$\sum Y_i = n\hat{a} + \hat{b} \sum X_{1i} + \hat{c} \sum X_{2i}$$

$$\sum X_{1i}Y_i = \hat{a}\sum X_{1i} + \hat{b}\sum X_{1i}^2 + \hat{c}\sum X_{1i}X_{2i}$$

and

$$\sum X_{2i} Y_i = \hat{a}\sum X_{2i} + \hat{b}\sum X_{1i} X_{2i} + \hat{c}\sum X_{2\,i}^2.$$

Solving for $\hat{a}$, $\hat{b}$, and $\hat{c}$, and using deviations from the mean such that

$$x_{1i} = X_{1i} - \overline{X}_1$$
$$x_{2i} = X_{2i} - \overline{X}_2$$

and

$$y_i = Y_i - \overline{Y},$$

we obtain

$$\hat{b} = \frac{\left(\sum x_1 y\right)\left(\sum x_2^2\right) - \left(\sum x_2 y\right)\left(\sum x_1 x_2\right)}{\left(\sum x_1^2\right)\left(\sum x_2^2\right) - \left(\sum x_1 x_2\right)^2} \qquad (3\text{-}43)$$

$$\hat{c} = \frac{\left(\sum x_2 y\right)\left(\sum x_1^2\right) - \left(\sum x_1 y\right)\left(\sum x_1 x_2\right)}{\left(\sum x_1^2\right)\left(\sum x_2^2\right) - \left(\sum x_1 x_2\right)^2} \qquad (3\text{-}44)$$

and

$$\hat{a} = \overline{Y} - \hat{b}\overline{X}_1 - \hat{c}\overline{X}_2. \qquad (3\text{-}45)$$

The variances of regression coefficients are

$$S_{\hat{b}}^2 = \frac{\sum(y - bx_1 - cx_2)^2}{(n-3)\sum(x_1 - d_1 x_2)^2} = \frac{\sum e_i^2}{(n-3)\sum v_1^2} \qquad (3\text{-}46)$$

and

$$S_{\hat{c}}^2 = \frac{\sum(y - b_1 x_1 - cx_2)^2}{(n-3)\sum(x_2 - d_2 x_1)^2} = \frac{\sum e_i^2}{(n-3)\sum v_2^2}, \qquad (3\text{-}47)$$

where v_1 is the unexplained residual in X_1 when X_1 is regressed on X_2, d_1 is the regression coefficient between X_1 and X_2, v_2 is the unexplained residual in X_2 when X_2 is regressed on X_1, and d_2 is the regression coefficient between X_2 and X_1.

Single-Equation Regression Model

When a model has more than two variables, we may ask whether the correlation between Y and X_1 is primarily due to the fact that each is influenced by the third variable X_2 or whether there is a significant net correlation between Y and X_1. Thus, the partial correlation coefficient is a measure of net correlation between two variables excluding the common influence of other variables in the equation. This statistical concept is equivalent to the concept of *ceteris paribus* used in economic literature.

Suppose that we want to calculate the partial-correlation coefficient between Y and X_1, with X_2 held constant, $\gamma_{01 \cdot 2}$. First we should eliminate the influence of X_2 from Y and from X_1. Let the linear regression of Y on X_2 be expressed as

$$Y_i = a_0 + c_0 X_{2i} + W_{0i}$$

and let

$$X_{1i} = a_1 + c_1 X_{2i} + W_{1i}$$

using terms of the deviation from mean,

$$W_{0i} = y_i - c_0 x_{2i}$$

and

$$W_{1i} = x_{1i} - c_1 x_{2i}.$$

The partial-correlation coefficient between Y and X_1, with X_2 held constant, then can be formulated as

$$
\begin{aligned}
\gamma_{01 \cdot 2} &= \frac{\sum W_{0i} W_{1i}}{\sqrt{\sum W_{0i}^2}\, \sqrt{\sum W_{1i}^2}} \\[2mm]
&= \frac{\sum (y_i - c_0 x_{2i})(x_{1i} - c_1 x_{2i})}{\sqrt{\sum (y_i - c_0 x_{2i})^2}\, \sqrt{\sum (x_{1i} - c_1 x_{2i})^2}}.
\end{aligned}
$$

(3-48)

Similarly, the partial-correlation coefficient between Y and X_2, with X_1 held constant, and the partial-correlation coefficient between X_1 and X_2, with Y held constant, can be obtained.

3.5.2   Statistical Inference in Three-Variable Model

The estimation of σ^2 in a three-variable case is exactly the same as in a two-variable case except that the degrees of freedom change from $n - 2$ into $n - 3$. The interval estimation and significance tests for regression coefficients are also identical to the two-variable model.

From Equation (3-38) it is understood that the increase additional variable in the equation will increase or at least not decrease the value of SSR, since sums of squares cannot be negative. R^2 obtained from the three-variable model has two parts: the proportion of variation in Y explained in X_1 alone plus the net additional proportion of the variation in Y explained in X_2 after controlling for X_1.†   Therefore, R^2 obtained from an equation with an additional variable will be at least equal to or larger than R^2 without the additional variable.

R^2 is often used as one of the criterion to judge the goodness of fit among several alternative functions. However, the argument above can always help us to obtain a relatively high R^2 if we increase additional variables in the equation. To account for a function having a higher number of explanatory variables, the adjusted coefficient of determination $\overline{R}^2$ is used:

$$\overline{R}^2 = 1 - (1 - R^2)\frac{n - 1}{n - k}, \qquad (3\text{-}49)$$

where n is number of observations in the equation and k is number of parameters in the equation. It can be seen that as n becomes large, the differences between $\overline{R}^2$ and R^2 tend to be small.

Following is a numerical example for a three-variable case.

Y	X_1	X_2	$y = Y - \overline{Y}$	$x_1 = X_1 - \overline{X}_1$	$x_2 = X_2 - \overline{X}_2$
40	4	8	-22	-4	-0.4
60	6	12	-2	-2	3.6
50	7	10	-12	-1	1.6
70	10	5	8	2	-3.4
90	13	7	28	5	-1.4

†For the algebraic proof see Goldberger, *Topics in Regression Analysis* (New York, Macmillan, 1968), pp. 42–45.

Single-Equation Regression Model

The information above gives us

$$n = 5 \qquad \sum Y = 310 \qquad \sum X_1 = 40 \qquad \sum X_2 = 42$$

$$\sum x_1 y = 260 \qquad \sum x_2 y = -84 \qquad \sum x_1 x_2 = -21$$

$$\sum x_1^2 = 50 \qquad \sum x_2^2 = 29.70 \qquad \sum y^2 = 1480.$$

Therefore,

$$\hat{b} = \frac{(260)(29.70) - (-84)(-21)}{(50)(29.70) - (-21)^2} = 5.72$$

$$\hat{c} = \frac{(-84)(50) - (260)(-21)}{(50)(29.70) - (-21)^2} = 1.24$$

$$\hat{a} = \overline{Y} - 5.72\overline{X}_1 - 1.24\overline{X}_2 = 5.86$$

$$SSE = \sum e^2$$

$$= (1.37)^2 + (4.99)^2 + (-8.26)^2 + (0.76)^2 + (1.13)^2$$

$$= 96.84,$$

so that

$$S = \sqrt{\frac{\sum e^2}{5 - 3}} = \sqrt{\frac{96.84}{2}} = 6.96$$

$$S_{\hat{b}} = \sqrt{\frac{\sum e^2}{(n - 3) \sum V_1^2}} = \sqrt{\frac{48.42}{34.81}} = 1.18$$

see Equation (3-46)

$$S_{\hat{c}} = \sqrt{\frac{\sum e^2}{(n - 3) \sum V_2^2}} = \sqrt{\frac{48.42}{20.25}} = 1.54$$

see Equation (3-47).

Thus the estimated equation can be summarized as

$$\hat{Y} = 5.86 + 5.72X_1 + 1.24X_2,$$
$$\phantom{\hat{Y} = 5.86 + } (1.18) \qquad (1.54)$$

where the value in parentheses is the standard error of the coefficient. From this equation we can compute

$$SSR = \sum \hat{y}^2 = 1383.16$$

$$SST = \sum y^2 = 1480.00$$

and

$$R^2 = \frac{SSR}{SST} = \frac{1383.16}{1480.00} = 0.93$$

$$\bar{R}^2 = 1 - (1 - 0.93)\frac{5 - 1}{5 - 3} = 0.86.$$

Finally, the test of significance of R^2 is provided by F ratio

$$F_{(2,2)} = \frac{SSR/(k - 1)}{SSE/(n - k)} = \frac{1383.16/2}{96.84/2} = 14.28.$$

This F ratio is a test of significance of both explanatory variables simutaneously.

3.5.3 More Than Three-Variable Model

So far the discussions are focused on a three-variable regression model. The statistical estimation of a more than three-variable model will be similar but algebraically more complicated. The computation will be simplified if we use matrix algebra.†

A Gauss–Dolittle method can show the solution of a normal equation when a model has more than three variables. The solution process may be viewed as a systematic method of solving a simultaneous equation system by substitution and elimination. Interested students may read the explanation in Goldberger's book.‡

†Those who have a knowledge of matrix algebra should consult the econometric textbook by Goldberger, *Econometric Theory* (New York, Wiley, 1964), chap. 4; or Johnston, *op. cit.*, chap. 4.
‡Goldberger, *Econometric Theory*, pp. 187–191.

4

FUNCTIONAL FORMS OF SINGLE-EQUATION REGRESSION MODEL

4.1 Conventional Functional Forms

The exact functional forms of quantitative relationships in econometric studies are rarely deduced theoretically; they are usually determined empirically. The simplest functional form is a linear equation, which is easiest to estimate and explain. In addition, basic statistical theory is developed primarily for linear equations.

However, economic relationships cannot always be expressed in linear form. In some cases an exponential or a logarithmic function best describes the curvature of the economic relationship. Since these functional forms can be easily transformed into the convenient linear form, exponential or logarithmic functions are also widely used in econometrics. The following are equation forms most commonly used in econometric analysis.

1. $Y = a + bX$ linear   (4-1)
2. $Y = a + bX + cX^2$ quadratic   (4-2)
3. $Y = a + b/X$ hyperbolic   (4-3)
4. $\log Y = a + bX$ semilogarithmic   (4-4)
5. $\log Y = \log a + b \log X$ doublelogarithmic   (4-5)
6. $Y = \log a + b \log X$ semilogarithmic   (4-6)

Each of these equations can be used to represent a certain type of curve. The variable on the left side of the equation (Y) is called the *dependent* variable, whereas the right side variable (X) is called the explanatory, or *independent*, variable. For instance, if we consider a consumption function, the dependent variable Y will represent per capita consumption, and the explanatory variable X will

4.1 Conventional Functional Forms

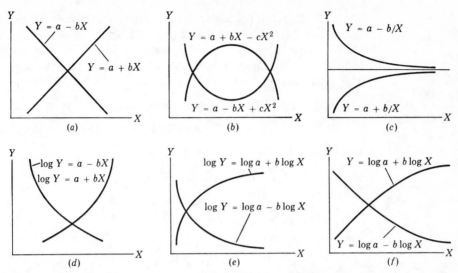

Figure 4-1 The shapes of the curves for various functional forms: (a) linear; (b) quadratic; (c) hyperbolic; (d) semilogarithmic; (e) doublelogarithmic; and (f) semilogarithmic.

represent per capita income. The coefficients a, b, and c are called parameters. The shapes of the curves for the equations above are illustrated in Figure 4-1.

Here are a few words about the applications of these functional forms in econometric studies. For instance, the simple consumption function is in a linear form, as expressed by Equation (4-1), in which consumption Y is a function of income X. The coefficient b is the marginal propensity to consume.

The quadratic form is sometimes used to relate a U-shaped average cost function in which average cost Y is a function of the level of output X and X^2. In order to have a U-shaped cost function we would assume that $b < 0$ and $c > 0$.

A hyperbolic function can be used to estimate an Engel curve that is a relationship between expenditures on a particular commodity Y and income X. This type of function is appropriate since economic theory suggests that there is a saturation level of expenditures on a given commodity and a minimum level of income to buy a given commodity. Semilog functions are also used quite often in empirical studies of Engel curves, which implies that the rate of increase of an individual's expenditures on a given commodity will be decreasing as income increases.

61

The doublelog functions are employed in the estimation of demand functions and production functions. One of the advantages of the doublelog function is that the coefficient of the independent variable X is also an elasticity of Y with respect to X. This property is shown as follows.

Equation (4-5) can be expressed alternatively by

$$Y = aX^b.$$

The elasticity of Y with respect to X is

$$\frac{X}{Y}\frac{dY}{dX} = \frac{X}{aX^b} \cdot abX^{b-1} = b.$$

Hence this elasticity is equal to

$$\frac{d \log Y}{d \log X} = b.$$

The concept of elasticity is a very important term that we discuss in the application of regression analysis in Chapter 6. A summary of Equations (4-1) through (4-6) with respect to the slope and the elasticities of the functions follows.

Name	Form	Slope ($\Delta Y/\Delta X$)	Elasticity
Linear	$Y = a + bX$	b	bX/Y
Quadratic	$Y = a + bX + cX^2$	$b + 2cX$	$(b + 2cX)\,X/Y$
Hyperbolic	$Y = a + b/X$	$-b/X^2$	$-b/XY$
Semilogrithmic	$\log Y = a + bX$	bY	bX
Doublelogrithmic	$\log Y = \log a + b \log X$	bY/X	b
Semilogrithmic	$Y = \log a + b \log X$	b/X	b/Y

4.2   Choice of Functional Form

As we have seen in the previous section, there are a number of alternative functional forms from which to choose in a particular econometric model. No definite rule cites which form is the appropriate one for a given problem. Econometricians have to decide this for themselves in each empirical study. Out of these experiences in decision-making for the functional form there may be some general criteria for a specific functional form.

Several criteria can be considered in choosing functional form. First, one tends to choose a *simple* form rather than a complicated form if the two can explain the problem equally well. Simplicity is the virtue of a theory. After all, a theory is an abstraction of the facts. The well-known economic theories, such as the law of demand and the Keynsian consumption function, are in their simplest forms. The virtue of simplicity has perhaps induced many researchers to rely upon the linear functions.

The second criterion is that one should rely on economic theory as much as possible in choosing functional forms. Indeed, the objective of econometrics is to give empirical content to economic theory. Fitting by various functional forms and choosing a "nice-looking" one without theoretical justification may induce one to admit that it is a measurement without theory. It would be simply a statistical exercise, not an econometric analysis.

The third criterion is that a "good" model should have "good" predictive power. After all, a model should not only summarize the actual economic phenomenon but also predict the future. This criterion suggests that the functional form should at least fit the data well; otherwise the chosen model will not have good predictive power.

All these three criteria are not necessarily consistent; they may contradict each other. Therefore, the choice of a functional form is often a difficult task for econometricians. Perhaps this is one of the reasons that Lawrence Klein said that econometrics is an art.

When we discussed the second and third criteria, we used the words "nice-looking" and "good." These can be evaluated by statistical judgment. A common agreement on the criterion of goodness-of-fit is to rely on $\bar{R}^2$, the adjusted R^2. The higher the value of $\bar{R}^2$, the larger the proportion of the dependent variable explained by a set of independent variables. The statistical significance of $\bar{R}^2$ can be tested by the F statistic, which is discussed in Section 3.4.

The other requirement for a nice-looking model is that the regression coefficients be statistically significant at the 1 or 5% level and that they have the expected sign or magnitudes. Of course, the judgment of expected signs or magnitudes is largely based on theoretical justification.

The statistical significance test of regression coefficients can also help us to choose the alternative functional

63

form. One obvious example is the choice between linear and quadratic forms. For instance

$$Y = a + bX + U_1 \qquad (4\text{-}7)$$

$$Y = a + bX + cX^2 + U_2 . \qquad (4\text{-}8)$$

The test of linearity is equivalent to testing the hypothesis that $c = 0$. On the other hand, the test of a quadratic form is equivalent to testing that $c \neq 0$.

Finally, there is another empirical analysis that can help us to decide a functional form. This analysis is the examination of the residual patterns. The error term in the true equation (3-1) is not observable. But the residuals (e_i) are defined as the differences between the observed dependent variables (Y_i) and their corresponding estimated dependent variables $(\hat{Y}_i)$:

$$e_i = Y_i - \hat{Y}_i . \qquad (4\text{-}9)$$

By this definition we can see that residuals are the amount of Y_i that have not been explained by the specified regression model. Therefore, the patterns of residuals can provide two kinds of information about the appropriateness of the regression model. Based on the patterns of residuals, we know whether or not the specified regression has missed any important variable. Also, the patterns of residuals suggest whether or not our specified functional form is appropriate. These can be illustrated by a number of examples.

The usual assumptions about the error terms are that they are independent of each other and have 0 mean and a constant variance. Thus if the model is fitted correctly, the residuals should tend to have no special pattern but to occur randomly, such as in Figure 4-2(a), in which the plot of residuals against the dependent variable is randomly scattered. Plotting the residuals against the observed dependent variable is the most common way of examining the residuals pattern. Of course, one can plot residuals against an independent variable or the estimated dependent variable.

If the pattern of residuals is similar to that shown in Figure 4-2(b), then we know that a time-trend variable (if the data are in time-series) or a size variable (if the data are in cross-section such as firms or households) should have been included in the regression mode. Figure 4-2(c) sug-

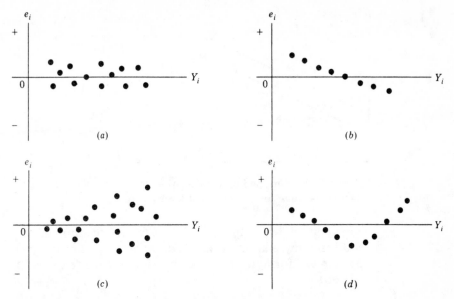

Figure 4-2 The various patterns of residuals: (a) random residuals; (b) linear-trend residuals; (c) nonconstant-variance residuals; and (d) U-shaped residuals.

gests that the variance of the error term is not constant but increases or decreases with the dependent variable. Thus a modification of the assumption for the variance of the error term is required. The method of modification is discussed in Section 5.3.

Finally, if the residual pattern shows a U or ∩ shape, as in Figure 4-2(d), then a linear-regression equation does not fit the data properly. One should consider a regression model with a linear and quadratic term of the independent variable.

4.3 Qualitative Independent Variables—
Dummy Variables

It is quite common in econometric research for many variables to be classified as categories or in a qualitative sense, such as race, sex, occupation, region, seasons, or wartime as against peacetime. Most commonly these variables are included in the regression analysis by creation of a categorical variable or dummy variable (also known as a binary variable) to dichotomize these variables that are not directly quantifiable. For example, one may be interested

65

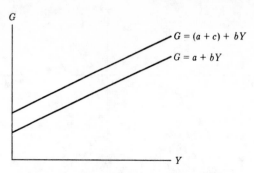

Figure 4-3 Wartime and peacetime government
expenditures functions by different levels.

in examining the impact of the war on government expenditures in relation to national income. A linear function can be formulated for a time-series data from 1954
to 1968:

$$G = a + bY + cW + U, \qquad (4\text{-}10)$$

where

G = government expenditures,
Y = national income,
$W = 1$ for wartime years (1965 through 1968),
$W = 0$ otherwise.

This equation is equivalent to the two separate equations,
one for the wartime-government expenditures function and
one for the peacetime-government expenditures function:

$$G = a + bY + c + U \qquad \text{for wartime}$$

and

$$G = a + bY + U \qquad \text{for peacetime.}$$

The variable W is called a dummy variable. In this case we
are assuming that these two functions have the same slope
but different intercepts. If we assume that $c > 0$, then
these two equations can be illustrated by Figure 4-3.

If we believe that not only the level of government
expenditures but also the slope of the expenditures will be
different in wartime and peacetime, then we should fit

$$G = \alpha + \beta Y + \gamma W + \delta Z + U, \qquad (4\text{-}11)$$

where $Z = WY$; that is, $Z = Y$ for war years and $= 0$ otherwise. This function again represents two different
equations:

$$G = \alpha + \beta Y + \gamma + \delta Y + U$$
$$= (\alpha + \gamma) + (\beta + \delta) Y + U \qquad \text{for wartime}$$

and

$$G = \alpha + \beta Y + U \qquad \text{for peacetime.}$$

If we assume that $\gamma > 0$ and $\delta > 0$, then these two equations can be illustrated by Figure 4-4.

The example above is for two classifications (war versus peace). We can also use dummy variables for more than two classifications, such as in the case of seasonal variation in retail sales or regional variation in personal incomes. For example,

$$Y = aX_1 + bX_2 + cX_3 + dX_4 + U, \qquad \text{(4-12)}$$

where Y = sales or income and the X's can be defined as follows.

	X_1	X_2	X_3	X_4
Winter (or east)	1	0	0	0
Spring (or north)	0	1	0	0
Summer (or west)	0	0	1	0
Fall (or south)	0	0	0	1

Each regression coefficient represents the level of sales (or income) for each season (or region). Figure 4-5 illustrates the meaning of the regression coefficient for a set of dummy variables. In this figure we assume that sales in

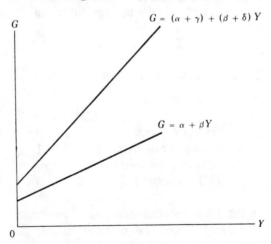

Figure 4-4 Wartime and peacetime government expenditures functions by different levels and slopes.

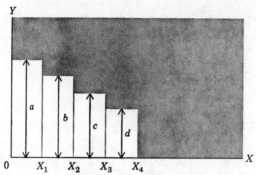

Figure 4-5 Illustrations of the regression coefficients for a set of dummy variables

winter (X_1) are higher than in spring (X_2), sales in spring (X_2) are higher than in summer (X_3), and sales in summer (X_3) are higher than in fall (X_4). Or, in terms of personal incomes, incomes in the east (X_1) are higher than in the north (X_2), incomes in the north (X_2) are higher than in the west (X_3), and incomes in the west (X_3) are higher than in the south (X_4).

An alternative way to introduce the dummy variable is to pick one of the categories as a base for comparison to other categories. This is equivalent to retaining a constant term in the regression equation, with the deleted category considered as a base. Suppose that we would like to measure the seasonal (or regional) effects relative to the winter (or the east). We set up the following equation:

$$Y = \alpha X_1 + \beta X_2 + \gamma X_3 + \delta X_4 + \mu. \qquad (4\text{-}13)$$

The X's are defined as follows:

	X_1	X_2	X_3	X_4
Winter (or east)	1	0	0	0
Spring (or north)	1	1	0	0
Summer (or west)	1	0	1	0
Fall (or south)	1	0	0	1

Figure 4-6 shows the meaning of the regression coefficients. β, γ, and δ are the differences of all other seasons (or regions) as against the winter (or the east). This is the most common approach in specifying a regression model—deleting one category and retaining a constant term.

4.3 Qualitative Independent Variables

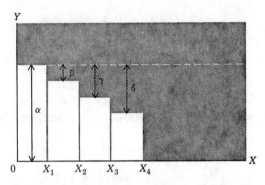

Figure 4-6 The relative differences of X_2, X_3, and X_4 with respect to X_1.

It should be noted that one cannot retain a whole set of dummy variables while still keeping the constant term in the equation. This implies that there are two identical variables in the equation and that the normal equation of the regression model cannot provide a unique solution. A review of Section 3.6.1 shows that this case implies that there are two equations and three unknowns. Thus the normal equations have infinitely many solutions. This is equivalent to the example shown in Section 5.1 for the extreme case of multicollinearity.

In a survey data analysis we are very likely to use more than one set of dummy variables. This can be done with no more complications. An illustration from a study by this author and his colleagues (1971) on labor-market performance of noncollege high school graduates follows. Consider the equation:

$$Y = 229 + 43X_1 + 12X_2 - 20X_3 + 137X_4 - 0.5X_5 + 76X_6$$
$$\quad\;\; (6) \quad\;\; (8) \quad\;\; (7) \quad\;\;\; (6) \quad\;\; (0.3) \quad\;\; (9)$$

$$\quad - 1X_7 - 4X_8 - 4X_9$$
$$\quad\;\; (7) \quad (14) \quad\; (0.9)$$

$$N = 2767 \qquad \bar{R}^2 = 0.20,$$

where N is the number of observations and $\bar{R}^2$ is the adjusted coefficient of determination. The values in parentheses are the standard errors of the coefficients. The variables are defined as follows:

Y = average, monthly, before-tax earnings in six years (1960 through 1966), in dollars
X_1 = 1 if vocational–technical graduates, 0 otherwise

69

$X_2 = 1$ if in city B, 0 otherwise
$X_3 = 1$ if in city C, 0 otherwise
$X_4 = 1$ if male, 0 otherwise
$X_5 = $ IQ scores, in points
$X_6 = 1$ if white, 0 otherwise
$X_7 = 1$ if single, 0 otherwise
$X_8 = 1$ if separated, widowed, or divorced, 0 otherwise
$X_9 = $ father's education, in years

In this example, variable X_1 indicates that vocational-technical graduates earn \$43 more monthly than non-vocational–technical high school graduates. Variable X_4 shows that male graduates earned \$137 more than the female graduates. Further, variable X_6 suggests that white graduates earned \$76 more monthly than nonwhite graduates, holding other factors are the same.

4.4 Qualitative Dependent Variables

If qualitative variables can appear as independent variables in the regression model, it must also be possible for qualitative variables to be dependent variables. Econometric researchers are interested in the factors determining an individual's behavior. For example, one either does or does not own a car, one does or does not own a house, or one does or does not graduate from college. Therefore, this dependent variable can take only two values, 1 or 0. Usually we use 1 if an event occurs and 0 if an event does not occur. This kind of function is also called a discriminate function. The predicted value of the dependent variable may be between 0 and 1 (it may also be larger than 1 or negative if we do not place restrictions on the range of variation of the dependent variable), and therefore, it is also known as the probability function.

An example of this kind of function can be illustrated by a sample shown in de Janosi's study of the demand for new automobiles based on household-survey data in 1952.[†] The estimated equation is

$$\hat{Y} = -0.008 + 0.0022X,$$

[†]de Janosi, *Factors Influencing the Demand for New Automobiles: A Cross-Section Analysis* (doctoral dissertation, Ann Arbor, Michigan, University of Michigan, 1956).

where

Y = 1 for purchase of new automobile, 0 otherwise;

X = disposable income in hundreds of dollars.

Thus for an individual with $20,000 disposable income, the probability of buying a new car is $-0.008 + 0.0022(200) = 0.432$. This kind of probability function has been used extensively for the prediction of consumer spending. An example of such predictions can be found in *Consumer Buying Prospects* (1966). The dependent variable used in this publication is a continuous scale of probabilities from 100% (absolutely certain) through 0% (absolutely no chance).

There are two drawbacks to the discriminate functions: One is that the classical assumption of the constant variance of the error term is no longer valid. A two-variable model can show this case. We define

$$e_i = Y_i - bX_i \qquad i = 1, 2, \ldots, n,$$

and when $Y_i = 0$, $e_i = -bX_i$; $Y_i = 1$, $e_i = 1 - bX_i$. Since $E(e_i) = 0$, by Equation (2-10) the expectation of e_i can be written as

$$E(e_i) = \sum e_i f(e_i)$$

$$= -bX_i(1 - bX_i) + (1 - bX_i)\, bX_i$$
$$= 0.$$

The variance of e_i can be expressed by Equation (2-12) as

$$V(e_i) = \sum (e_i)^2\, f(e_i)$$

$$= (-bX_i)^2\, (1 - bX_i) + (1 - bX_i)^2\, (-bX_i)$$
$$= (bX_i)\, (1 - bX_i)$$
$$= EY_i(1 - EY_i). \qquad (4\text{-}14)$$

Thus the variance of the error term is not a constant but varies with the dependent variable Y_i or X_i. The result of this derivation implies that the classical least-squares method is not appropriate to the probability-function estimation. As we shall see in Section 5.3, the violation of the constant-variance assumption of the error term causes the variance of the regression coefficient to no longer be the minimum. The method of correction for this case is shown in Section 5.3.

The second limitation of the discriminate function is that the predicted value of the dependent variable may fall outside of the interval between 0 and 1, which is inconsistent with the definition of probability. One simple way to overcome this is to set critical values for the values of 0 and 1, such as in Lee's study of the probability of installment borrowing by durable-goods buyers.[†] In the study he grouped those $\hat{Y}_i < 0$ in the $0 \leqslant Y_i \leqslant 0.1$ category, and those with $\hat{Y}_i > 1.0$ were grouped with the $0.9 \leqslant \hat{Y}_i \leqslant 1.0$ category, where $\hat{Y}_i$ was the predicted probability of installment borrowing. A more comprehensive way of handling this problem is shown in Tobin's work.[‡]

[†]Lee, "An Analysis of Installment Borrowing by Durable Goods Buyers," *Econometrica*, Vol. 30 (October 1962), pp. 770–787.

[‡]Tobin, "Estimation of Relationships for Limited Dependent Variables," *Econometrica*, Vol. 26 (January 1958), pp. 24–36.

5

PROBLEMS IN
SINGLE-EQUATION
REGRESSION ESTIMATION

5.1 Multicollinearity

5.1.1 Causes and Effects

Multicollinearity is a phenomenon that occurs in a regression model when two or more independent variables tend to move together in the same pattern. In other words, the variables are so highly correlated that it is difficult to separate their respective effects on the dependent variable. This phenomenon can be best illustrated by a typical example of a demand function in which price and income variables are highly correlated, since both price and income are likely to be moving together over the business cycle.

Multicollinearity occurs not only in time-series data but also in cross-section samples. For instance, when we use capital and labor data in the estimation of a production function, we will find that capital and labor are highly correlated, since a relatively large firm tends to have a larger amount of capital assets and labor forces, and a relatively small firm tends to have a small amount of capital assets and labor forces.

An extremely severe case of multicollinearity occurs when two variables are perfectly correlated. In a three-variable case we can illustrate the effect of a perfect multicollinearity. Suppose that

$$Y = a + bX_1 + cX_2 + U$$

and $X_1 = KX_2$. The least-squares estimates of b and c according to Equations (3-43) and (3-44) are

$$\hat{b} = \frac{(\sum x_1 y)(\sum x_2{}^2) - (\sum x_2 y)(\sum x_1 x_2)}{(\sum x_1{}^2)(\sum x_2{}^2) - (\sum x_1 x_2)^2}$$

$$\hat{c} = \frac{\left(\sum x_2 y\right) \left(\sum x_1{}^2\right) - \left(\sum x_1 y\right) \left(\sum x_1 x_2\right)}{\left(\sum x_1{}^2\right) \left(\sum x_2{}^2\right) - \left(\sum x_1 x_2\right)^2}$$

where b and c have a common denominator,

$$\sum(x_1{}^2) \left(\sum x_2{}^2\right) - \left(\sum x_1 x_2\right)^2 = \sum(x_1{}^2) \left(K^2 \sum x_1{}^2\right)$$
$$- \left(K \sum x_1{}^2\right)^2 = 0.$$

Therefore, when two independent variables are perfectly correlated, the solution for b and c are indeterminant. As we indicated in Section 4.3 that in this case, the normal equations have many solutions, not a unique solution.

The common case of multicollinearity is less extreme. But this will cause the standard error of the coefficient to be larger than it is in the case of no collinearity. This can be readily examined by Equations (3-46) and (3-47):

$$S_b^2 = \frac{\sum e_i^2}{(n - 3) \sum v_1{}^2}$$

and

$$S_c^2 = \frac{\sum e_i^2}{(n - 3) \sum v_2{}^2},$$

where v_1 is the unexplained residual in X_1 when X_1 is regressed on X_2, and v_2 is the unexplained residual in X_2 when X_2 is regressed on X_1. For high correlation between X_1 and X_2, both $\Sigma v_1{}^2$ and $\Sigma v_2{}^2$ tend to be small. Thus, the standard errors of b and c tend to be large when X_1 and X_2 are highly correlated. The high value of the standard error of the coefficient will result in an imprecision in the regression coefficient, which will result in not rejecting the null hypothesis in the regression analysis. When multicollinearity exists, the fit of the regression equation has usually resulted in high values of R^2, but there are no statistically significant coefficients different from 0.

So far we have discussed pair-wise correlation. In the case of more than three independent variables in the regression equation, the simple pair-wise correlation coefficient cannot indicate the degree of collinearity among a set of variables. However, Farrar and Glauber introduced a method to evaluate the degree of multicollinearity among a set of independent variables.† Interested students should consult their study.

5.1.2 Estimation Methods

There are a number of ways to overcome the problem of multicollinearity.

1. When the case of multicollinearity is severe, we may have to collect more data to reduce the multicollinearity. When we expand a longer time-series data or a wide range of cross-section data, the phenomenon of close association between two variables may be reduced.

2. Alternatively we can make use of theoretical information or information obtained from other data sources and then eliminate one of the two collinear variables. Suppose that we would like to estimate a production function

$$\log Q = a + b \log L + c \log K + U \qquad (5\text{-}1)$$

where Q is the total output, L is labor, and K is capital. If we find that $\log L$ and $\log K$ are highly correlated and if we assume that this production function has constant return to scale (Cobb–Douglas production function), then we may rewrite

$$\log Q = a + b \log L + (1 - b) \log K + U \qquad (5\text{-}2)$$

or

$$\log Q - \log K = a + b (\log L - \log K) + U, \qquad (5\text{-}3)$$

and then take the regression of $(\log Q - \log K)$ on $(\log L - \log K)$ to estimate b.

The other common approach is to use both time-series and cross-section data. This was first applied in a number of demand analyses by Wold and Jureen,‡ Stone,§ and Tobin.¶ Since price and income are highly

---

†Farrar and Glauber, "Multicollinearity in Regression Analysis: The Problem Revisited," *Review of Economics and Statistics*, Vol. 49 (February 1967), pp. 92–107.

‡Wold and Jureen, *Demand Analysis* (New York, Wiley, 1953).

§Stone, *The Measurement of Consumers' Expenditure and Behavior in the United Kingdom, 1928–1938* (Cambridge, Cambridge University Press, 1954).

¶Tobin, "A Statistical Demand Function for Food in the U.S.A.," *Journal of Royal Statistical Society*, Vol. 113 (1950), pp. 113–141.

correlated, we can make use of income elasticity from the cross-section data to estimate the price elasticity from the time-series data. The example can be illustrated as follows:

$$Q_t = a + bY_t + cP_t + U_t \qquad t = 1, 2, \ldots, T, \qquad (5\text{-}4)$$

where Q is the quantity demanded, Y is disposable income, P is the price, and t denotes the time period. Since Y and P are highly correlated, we may use cross-section data to estimate

$$Q_i = \alpha + \beta Y_i + U_i \qquad i = 1, 2, \ldots, n, \qquad (5\text{-}5)$$

where i denotes the individual households. We estimate Equation (5-5) first and then assume that $\hat{\beta}$ is an unbiased estimate of b. Then the revised time-series demand function becomes

$$Q_t - \hat{\beta} Y_t = a + cP_t + U_t . \qquad (5\text{-}6)$$

Finally, $Q_t - \hat{\beta} Y_t$ is regressed on P_t based on the time-series data. This approach is called extraneous-information estimation. In most cases this estimation is used not only to overcome the multicollinearity problem but also to reduce the standard error of the coefficient. The simplest explanation is that the degrees of freedom are increased to estimate the standard error of the estimate and, in turn, to reduce the standard error of the coefficient. Detailed statistical proofs are shown in Goldberger.†

3. The other alternative is to change the functional form. In certain nonlinear functional forms, such as the quadratic form X and X^2, X and X^2 may be highly correlated. This is true especially if the ranges of X's and Y's are relatively short. In this case one may simply drop the X^2 term and just use the linear form to approximate the nonlinear curve.

4. The last alternative is, of course, to either leave the variables in the function or to drop one of them from the model. This again depends on the objective of the study. If the objective is to predict or forecast, then multicollinearity may not cause a serious problem. Also, if there is no other information provided that

---

†Goldberger, *Econometric Theory* (New York, Wiley, 1964), pp. 255–265.

would warrant dropping one of the variables or if economic theory suggests that the variable should be included in the function, then one may have to leave the variable in the equation although it contributes to the multicollinearity problem. After all, there is no clear-cut way to solve the multicollinearity phenomenon. It is simply inherent in the economic data, and one always has to keep this problem in mind.

5.2 Autocorrelation

5.2.1 Causes and Effects

One of the assumptions of the classical least-squares model stated in Section 3.1 is that the disturbance terms are obtained independently of one another; that is,

$$E(U_i U_j) = 0 \quad \text{for } i \neq j, 1, 2, \ldots, n .$$

However, this assumption may not be realistic, especially in a time-series analysis in which the error term is correlated with its own past value. In other words, the error term can be expressed as a function of its past values. It also may occur in the cross-section analysis, where if we arrange the dependent variable by the order of its magnitude, then corresponding error terms may be correlated with each other.

Several sources can cause autocorrelation. For example, when one omits a certain variable in the regression equation, the error term may represent the influence of the omitted variable. One obvious case is the time-trend variable that we illustrated in Section 4.2. Another example would be misspecification of the functional form of the regression model. If we specify a linear form between Y and X and if in fact the relation should include X and X^2, then the error term may contain the factor of X^2. And if X is autocorrelated in nature, then the error term will be autocorrelated.

Serial correlation is an alternative term for autocorrelation. These terms are often interchangeable, but if one wants to make the distinction between them he may say that if observations are ordered in time and if they are correlated in time sequence, this is serial correlation. On the

Problems in Single-Equation Regression Estimation

other hand, autocorrelation is not necessarily confined to time-series but may refer to cross-section as well.

The effects of autocorrelation can be examined by a two-variable case:

$$Y_t = a + bX_t + U_t ,\qquad (5\text{-}7)$$

where we assume that U_t is a linear function of U_{t-1}.

$$U_t = \rho U_{t-1} + e_t ,\qquad (5\text{-}8)$$

where $-1 < \rho < 1$, and

$$E(e_t) = 0 \qquad (5\text{-}9)$$

$$E(e_t e_{t+i}) = \sigma_e^2 \qquad \text{when } i = 0 \text{ for all } t \qquad (5\text{-}10)$$

and

$$E(e_t e_{t+i}) = 0 \qquad \text{when } i \neq 0 \text{ for all } t. \qquad (5\text{-}11)$$

Successive substitution in Equation (5-8) results in

$$
\begin{aligned}
U_t &= \rho U_{t-1} + e_t \\
&= \rho(\rho U_{t-2} + e_{t-1}) + e_t \\
&= e_t + \rho e_{t-1} + \rho^2 e_{t-2} + \rho^3 e_{t-3} + \cdots \qquad (5\text{-}12)
\end{aligned}
$$

then $E(U_t) = 0$, and

$$
\begin{aligned}
V(U_t) &= E[U_t - E(U_t)]^2 \\
&= E(U_t)^2 \\
&= E(e_t^2) + \rho^2 E(e_{t-1}^2) + \rho^4 E(e_{t-2}^2) + \cdots
\end{aligned}
$$

$$\text{by Equation (5-11)}$$

$$= (1 + \rho^2 + \rho^4 + \cdots)\sigma_e^2$$

$$\text{by Equation (5-10)} . \qquad (5\text{-}13)$$

We define $V(U_t) = \sigma^2$, and since $-1 < \rho < 1$, Equation (5-13) can be rewritten as

$$\sigma^2 = \left(\frac{1}{1-\rho^2}\right)\sigma_e^2 . \qquad (5\text{-}14)$$

Since $0 < \rho^2 < 1$, then $[1/(1-\rho^2)] > 0$. Therefore,

$$\sigma^2 > \sigma_e^2 , \qquad (5\text{-}15)$$

where σ^2 is the variance of the autocorrelated error term and σ_e^2 is the variance of the nonautocorrelated error term. In other words, when there is no autocorrelation $\rho = 0$, and the error term of Equation (5-7) should be e_t.

We conclude that autocorrelation tends to make the variance of the error term (or the standard error of the estimate) relatively large. This, in turn, will cause a larger standard error of the coefficient, which leads to inefficient estimation.

According to Equation (5-8), we can also show that the covariance of U_t and U_{t-1} in fact does not equal 0, so that they are not independent of each other.

$$E(U_t U_{t-1}) = E(e_t + \rho e_{t-1} + \rho^2 e_{t-2} + \cdots)(e_{t-1} + \rho e_{t-2}$$
$$+ \rho^2 e_{t-3} + \cdots)$$
$$= E[e_t + \rho(e_{t-1} + \rho e_{t-2} + \cdots)](e_{t-1} + \rho e_{t-2}$$
$$+ \rho^2 e_{t-3})$$
$$= \rho E[(e_{t-1} + \rho e_{t-2} + \rho^2 e_{t-3} + \cdots)^2]$$
$$= \rho \sigma^2$$
$$\neq 0$$

5.2.2 Estimation Methods

We have to know how to detect the presence of an autocorrelated error term before we can make any corrections of autocorrelation. The most popular detective technique is the Durbin–Watson test of 1950 and 1951.

The null hypothesis of the Durbin–Watson test is that there is no autocorrelation among the error terms in the first-order condition. In other words, the null hypothesis is that ρ is equal to 0 in Equation (5-8). ρ is called the autocorrelation coefficient. The statistic used is

$$\text{DW} = \frac{\sum_{t=2}^{n} (\hat{u}_t - \hat{u}_{t-1})^2}{\sum_{t=1}^{n} \hat{u}_t^2}. \tag{5-16}$$

Durbin and Watson have provided tables for testing the serial correlation. In this test they have set the lower and upper critical values d_L and d_U for various values of the number of independent variables K' and sample size n as shown in Appendix B, Table 4. If $\text{DW} < d_L$, we reject the null hypothesis and accept the hypothesis of positive autocorrelation $\rho > 0$. If $\text{DW} > d_U$, we do not reject the null hypothesis. If $d_L < \text{DW} < d_U$, the test is inconclusive.

79

On the other hand, if DW $> 4 - d_L$, we reject the null hypothesis and accept the hypothesis of negative autocorrelation $\rho < 0$. If DW $< 4 - d_U$, we do not reject the null hypothesis. If $4 - d_U <$ DW $< 4 - d_L$, the test is inconclusive.

We use the annual United States per capita consumption and disposable-income data to estimate a consumption function from 1954 through 1964: $C = 4.42 + 0.9258\ Y_d$. Based upon this data, we can use the following example as an illustration of the application of the Durbin–Watson statistic.

Year	C_t	$\hat{C}_t$	$\hat{U}_t$	$\hat{U}_{t-1}$
1954	1682	1684.8	-2.8	
1955	1775	1759.8	15.2	-2.8
1956	1802	1815.4	-13.4	15.2
1957	1818	1826.5	-8.5	-13.4
1958	1805	1816.3	-11.3	-8.5
1959	1875	1870.0	5.0	-11.3
1960	1897	1875.5	21.5	5.0
1961	1902	1908.9	-6.9	21.5
1962	1963	1963.6	-0.5	-6.9
1963	2008	1999.6	8.4	-0.5
1964	2079	2085.7	-6.7	8.4

Based on $\hat{U}_t$, Equation (5-16) gives DW $= 2.259$. With $K' = 1$, $n = 15$ (we take this value because it is the lowest value the table has), $d_L = 0.95$, and $d_U = 1.23$. According to the criterion of rejection, we do not reject the null hypothesis.

Once we have observed autocorrelation in the error terms, we have to find various methods to overcome this problem. The methods can be summarized as follows.

1. If the assumption of the first-order autocorrelation is true, then as long as we can obtain ρ in Equation (5-8), we can rearrange Equation (5-7) and solve the autocorrelation problem. The justification follows:

$$Y_t = a + bX_t + U_t$$
$$= a + bX_t + \rho U_{t-1} + e_t.$$

Substituting $Y_{t-1} - a - bX_{t-1}$ for U_{t-1}, we obtain

$$Y_t = a + bX_t + \rho(Y_{t-1} - a - bX_{t-1}) + e_t$$

or

$$Y_t - \rho Y_{t-1} = a(1 - \rho) + b(X_t - \rho X_{t-1}) + e_t. \quad (5\text{-}17)$$

Equation (5-17) implies that the error term is serially uncorrelated; therefore, the classical least-squares estimate is efficient. Now the problem is how to obtain ρ.

Recall from Equation (5-8) that we can define ρ as the autocorrelation coefficient such that the estimate of ρ can be obtained from the following equation:

$$\hat{\rho} = \frac{\sum_{t=2}^{n} \hat{U}_t \hat{U}_{t-1}}{\sqrt{\sum_{t=2}^{n} \hat{U}_t^2} \sqrt{\sum_{t=2}^{n} \hat{U}_{t-1}^2}}. \quad (5\text{-}18)$$

Thus, the remedy of autocorrelation in this approach involves three steps. First, we use the classical least-squares approach to estimate Equation (5-7) and to obtain $\hat{U}_t$. Second, we use $\hat{U}_t$ to obtain $\hat{\rho}$ according to Equation (5-18). Finally, we have a new dependent variable $Y_t - \rho Y_{t-1}$ to regress on the new independent variable $X_t - \rho X_{t-1}$, and the parameters a and b can be obtained.

2. Since we know that ρ lies between -1 and 1, we may simply try to substitute ρ into Equation (5-17) from -1 to 1 at successive intervals of 0.1 and choose the estimated equation with the estimated DW statistic that does not reject the null hypothesis of autocorrelation. The simplest version of this approach is the "first-difference" method, which assumes that $\rho = 1$ in Equation (5-17). This approach is appropriate if ρ is in fact around the value of 1. It can be easily seen that the first-difference approach does not affect the regression coefficients.

3. An alternative two-step approach to overcome the autocorrelation, as suggested by Durbin,† is first to formulate

$$Y_t = a + bX_t + \rho Y_{t-1} + U_t, \quad (5\text{-}19)$$

†Durbin, "Estimation of Parameters in Time-Series Regression Models," *Journal of the Royal Statistical Society*, Vol. 22, Series B (1960), pp. 139–153.

and then to apply the classical least-squares estimation to obtain $\hat{\rho}$. Based on this $\hat{\rho}$, Equation (5-17) is estimated.

4. Finally, as we indicated in the Section 5.2.1, one of the sources of autocorrelation is a result of omitted variables in the regression model. This cause may be revealed in the residual pattern, such as a time-trend variable or a dummy variable for a certain block of observations. Therefore, an introduction of a new variable in the model may reduce the autocorrelation.

5.3   Heteroscedasticity

5.3.1   Causes and Effects

The classical least-squares approach assumes that the error terms are independently distributed with 0 mean and constant variance σ^2. However, the assumption of the constant variance may not always be valid. That is, it may happen that the errors are mutually uncorrelated and have different variances. If the residual patterns exhibit the form, as Figure 4-2(c) indicates, then the error terms are not constant. The existence of heteroscedasticity may often occur in the cross-section data. For example, the variance of savings among high-income families may be larger than the variance among low-income families. Also, the variance of investment expenditures among the large firms may be greater than the variance among the small firms.

The main effect of heteroscedasticity is not on the biasness of the estimated regression coefficient but on efficiency—the variance of the estimated regression coefficient. This effect can be demonstrated algebraically as follows:

$$Y_i = a + bX_i + U_i \qquad i = 1, 2, \ldots, n,$$

where

$$E(U_i) = 0$$

$$E(U_i U_j) = 0 \qquad \text{for } i \neq j$$

$$E(U_i^2) = K_i \sigma^2 \qquad i = 1, 2, \ldots, n.$$

The classical least-squares estimate of b will be the same as Equation (3-11):

$$\hat{b} = \frac{(\sum X_i)\ (\sum Y_i) - n\sum X_i Y_i}{(\sum X_i)^2 - n\sum X_i^2},$$

but the variance of $\hat{b}$ becomes

$$V(\hat{b}) = E(b - b)^2$$

$$= E\left(\frac{\sum x_i U_i}{\sum x_i^2}\right)^2$$

$$= E\left[\frac{1}{(\sum x_i^2)^2}\ (x_1^2 U_1^2 + x_2^2 U_2^2 + \cdots + x_n^2 U_n^2 \right.$$

$$\left. +2x_1 x_2 U_1 U_2 + \cdots + 2x_{n-1} x_n U_{n-1} U_n)\right]$$

$$= \frac{1}{(\sum x_i^2)^2}\ [x_1^2 E(U_1^2) + x_2^2 E(U_2^2) + \cdots$$

$$+ x_n^2 E(U_n^2)]$$

$$= \frac{\sigma^2}{(\sum x_i^2)^2}\ (K_1 x_1^2 + K_2 x_2^2 + \cdots + K_n x_n^2)$$

$$= \frac{\sigma^2}{(\sum x_i^2)} \cdot \frac{\sum K_i x_i^2}{\sum x_i^2}. \tag{5-20}$$

If K_i and x_i are positively correlated and $(\Sigma K_i x_i^2 / \Sigma x_i^2) > 1$, then the classical least-squares estimation for the variance of $\hat{b}$ will be overestimated. It is most likely that in economic data the residual variance is positively correlated with the independent variables such as the saving and income relations or the investment and firm-size relations.

5.3.2 Estimation Methods

Before we try to make any corrections for heteroscedasticity we should first try to detect the presence of heteroscedasticity in the error terms. Two common methods are used to test the heteroscedasticity of the variance.

1. We can plot the residuals against the dependent variable and examine the patterns of residuals. If the shape is similar to that in Figure 4-2(c), then there is a possibility of heteroscedasticity in the error terms.

2. A more careful method is to break the sample into two or more groups, each corresponding to a **single** value of the independent variable X, and then compute the error-variance for each group. Our null hypothesis is that there is no difference among the variances of these groups. To test this hypothesis we can use the chi-square test, as we discussed in Section 2.3.4, assuming that the error terms are normally distributed and independently distributed. However, the breakdown of these groups is rather arbitrary in terms of different ranges of X. Therefore, the test is viewed to be merely an indication of the presence of heteroscedasticity.

Once we have detected that there is heteroscedasticity in the error terms, we have to correct this problem.

To improve the efficiency of our estimates we should obtain the value of K_i and multiply all variables by $1/\sqrt{K_i}$ in each of the i'th observations.

$$Y_i \frac{1}{\sqrt{K_i}} = a \frac{1}{\sqrt{K_i}} + bX_i \frac{1}{\sqrt{K_i}} + U_i \frac{1}{\sqrt{K_i}}. \qquad (5\text{-}21)$$

The variance of Equation (5-21) is a constant value

$$E\left(U_i \frac{1}{\sqrt{K_i}}\right)^2 = \frac{1}{K_i} E(U_i^2) = \frac{1}{K_i}(K_i \sigma^2) = \sigma^2.$$

We then apply the classical least-squares estimation to Equation (5-21), and the estimates of the regression coefficients will be efficient. The equations for estimating the regression coefficient and the variance of the coefficient follow:

$$\hat{b} = \frac{\left(\sum 1/K_i\right)\left(\sum X_i Y_i \, 1/K_i\right) - \left(\sum X_i \, 1/K_i\right)\left(\sum Y_i \, 1/K_i\right)}{\left(\sum 1/K_i\right)\left(\sum X_i^2 \, 1/K_i\right) - \left(\sum X_i \, 1/K_i\right)^2},$$
$$(5\text{-}22)$$

$$V(\hat{b}) = \frac{\sigma^2 \sum\left(1/K_i\right)}{\left(\sum 1/K_i\right)\left(\sum X_i^2 \, 1/K_i\right) - \left(\sum X_i \, 1/K_i\right)^2}.$$
$$(5\text{-}23)$$

This method of correction in statistical theory is known as the generalized least-squares method, in which we estimate the regression coefficients, taking into account the nonhomogeneity of the variance. It is also often known as weighted regression, since the regression coefficients are obtained by weights that are assigned to each observation.

The empirical problem of this approach is how to obtain the values of K_i, or the weights. Two cases are usually used to estimate K_i. In budget studies it has been observed that high-income people have greater variability in their savings than do low-income people. Therefore, it often appears that the variance of the error terms is proportional to the square of income X_i^2; that is,

$$E(U_i^2) = \sigma^2 X_i^2.$$

Then if we use the technique indicated in Equation (5-21), we obtain

$$\frac{Y_i}{X_i} = a \frac{1}{X_i} + b + \frac{U_i}{X_i}. \tag{5-24}$$

Classical least-squares analysis can then be applied to Equation (5-24). In this case the marginal propensity to save is the constant term b in Equation (5-24).

In survey data, such as the 1960 Survey of Financial Characteristics of Consumers by the Federal Reserve System and the data collected by the University of Michigan Survey Research Center, consumers are sampled based on different probabilities among different consumer-income groups in order to ensure a large amount of wealthier consumer units in the sample. To avoid the biased estimated caused by the uneven proportional contribution of each group to the sample, the weights—the square roots of the reciprocals of the probabilities of selection for each observation—are adjusted, as shown by Equation (5-21). This means that those observations sampled at a relatively high rate are given a little weight in the regression analysis. Therefore, the weighted regression gives regression coefficients *as if* the sample were chosen with the same probability.

5.4 Errors in Variables

5.4.1 Causes and Effects

In the classical least-squares model we assume that sample observations are exactly measured. In other words, we assume that there are no errors of measurement in the variable. However, this assumption may not be realistic, since most published data or survey information contains errors of summarizing or reporting.

Where only one variable has possible errors in measurement the problem is very simple. One of the justifications of the **error** term in the regression equation is that there is **error of** measurement in the variable. For example,

$$Y = a + bX + U. \qquad (5\text{-}25)$$

If Y is the true value and if the observed value is Y^*, then

$$Y^* = Y + V, \qquad (5\text{-}26)$$

where V is the **error** in observed Y. Therefore, the actual estimation becomes

$$Y^* = a + bX + U^*, \qquad (5\text{-}27)$$

where $U^* = U + V$ is a new error term in Equation (5-27). The classical least-squares assumption is not violated.

If only the dependent variable X has an error of measurement, the solution is still straightforward. Let X be the true value and let the observed value be X^*; then

$$X^* = X + W. \qquad (5\text{-}28)$$

The regression model can be written as

$$X^* = c + dY + W, \qquad (5\text{-}29)$$

and d is equivalent to $1/b$. Again Equation (5-29) can be estimated by the classical least-squares method.

Suppose that both X and Y have errors of measurement such that

$$Y^* = Y + V$$

and

$$X^* = X + W,$$

where Y^* and X^* are the observed values, Y and X are the true values, and V and W are the errors in measurement. Let the true relation between Y and X be that shown in Equation (5-25). Inserting these two definitions into Equation (5-25) and rearranging gives

$$Y^* = a + bX^* + e, \qquad (5\text{-}30)$$

where $e = V - bW$. Even if we assume that both V and W have 0 mean, are mutually independent with constant variances, and also are independent of the true values of Y and X, $X*$ and e may still be correlated:

$$EX*e = E(X + W)(V - bW)$$
$$= E(XV) + E(WV) - E(XbW) - E(WbW)$$
$$= - b \operatorname{var}(W)$$
$$\neq 0, \tag{5-31}$$

since by above assumptions XV, WV, and XW are independent, respectively. Equation (5-31) is clearly violating one of the assumptions of the classical least-squares method. We can show that when $X*$ and e are correlated, the classical least-squares estimator of b will be biased even when the sample size increases. This is alternatively known as asymptotic biasness or inconsistency. Students may review these concepts in Section 2.3.1. The proof follows:

$$\hat{b} = \frac{\sum(X* - \bar{X}*)(Y* - \bar{Y}*)}{\sum(X* - \bar{X}*)^2}$$

$$= \left[\sum(X-\bar{X})(Y-\bar{Y}) + \sum(X-\bar{X})(V-\bar{V}) + \sum(Y-\bar{Y})(W-\bar{W}) + \sum(V+\bar{V})(W-\bar{W})\right] / \left[\sum(X-\bar{X})^2 + 2\sum(X-\bar{X})(W-\bar{W}) + \sum(W-\bar{W})^2\right].$$

If we divide by n (the number of observations) throughout the denominator and numerator, then, as the sample size n increases to infinity, the probability limiting value of $\hat{b}$ becomes

$$p \lim \hat{b} = \frac{\sum(X - \bar{X})(Y - \bar{Y})/n}{\sum(X - \bar{X})^2 /n + \sum(W - \bar{W})^2 /n}$$

$$= \frac{\hat{b}}{1 + V(W)/V(X)}. \tag{5-32}$$

Since by assumption XV, YW, and VW are independent, respectively, $\hat{b}$ is the true regression coefficient. Equation (5-32) implies that $p \lim \hat{b} < \hat{b}$, for variances are always nonnegative and $\left[\dfrac{1}{1 + V(W)/V(X)}\right] \leqslant 1$. In other words, when there are errors in the variables, the classical least-squares estimate of the regression coefficient will be an underestimate in comparison to the true regression coefficient.

A famous example of the errors in the variables in economic theory is the permanent-income hypothesis by Friedman.† Let Y be permanent consumption and let X be permanent income; then Friedman's permanent-consumption equation is

$$Y = bX + U. \qquad (5\text{-}33)$$

Then V is transitory consumption and W is transitory income; $Y*$ and $X*$ are measured or observed consumption and income, respectively. It is with this specification that Friedman suggests that the classical least-squares estimate of the marginal propensity to consume underestimates the true marginal propensity to consume according to Equation (5-32).

5.4.2 Estimation Methods

There are a number of ways to overcome the problem of errors in variables.

1. When both Y and X include errors, we may find a new variable Z that is independent of both errors V and W, but in which Z is correlated with X. This Z variable is called the instrumental variable.

$$X* = g + hZ + \theta. \qquad (5\text{-}34)$$

Then the estimate of h is

$$\hat{h} = \frac{\sum(X* - \bar{X}*)(Z - \bar{Z})}{\sum(Z - \bar{Z})^2}. \qquad (5\text{-}35)$$

When we substitute Equation (5-34) into Equation (5-30), we get

$$Y* = (a + bg) + bh\,Z + (e + b\theta). \qquad (5\text{-}36)$$

The least-squares estimator for bh is

$$\widehat{bh} = \frac{\sum(Y* - \bar{Y}*)(Z - \bar{Z})}{\sum(Z - \bar{Z})^2}. \qquad (5\text{-}37)$$

Comparing Equations (5-35) and (5-37), the estimate for b is

$$\hat{b} = \frac{\sum(Y* - \bar{Y}*)(Z - \bar{Z})}{\sum(X* - \bar{X}*)(Z - \bar{Z})}. \qquad (5\text{-}38)$$

---

†Friedman, *A Theory of the Consumption Function* (Princeton, Princeton University Press, 1957).

Equation (5-38) is called the instrumental-variable estimation. The instrumental-variable method provides a consistent estimator, since Z is uncorrelated with $e + b\theta$.

The use of instrumental-variable estimation is not necessarily limited to the case of errors in variables. In fact, this method can be used when the error term is correlated with the independent variable. However, a major problem arises from the use of an instrumental variable—the arbitrary nature of choosing an instrumental variable. Different instrumental variables yield different regression results, and the interpretation of the resultant estimates becomes difficult.

2. A simpler method of correction is suggested by Wald,[†] assuming that the errors of variables are serially and mutually independent. Assuming an even number of observations $n = 2k$ of the observed X and Y, X^* and Y^*, respectively. The X^* values are to be ordered in ascending magnitude, with Y^* corresponding to the respective X^*:

$$X_1^*, X_2^*, X_3^*, \ldots, X_k^*, X_{k+1}^*, X_{k+2}^*, \ldots, X_n^*$$

and

$$Y_1^*, Y_2^*, Y_3^*, \ldots, Y_k^*, Y_{k+1}^*, Y_{k+2}^*, \ldots, Y_n^*.$$

The subgroup means follow:

$$\overline{Y}_1^* = \frac{1}{K}\sum_{i=1}^{K} Y_i^* \qquad \overline{Y}_2^* = \frac{1}{K}\sum_{i=K+1}^{n} Y_i^*$$

$$\overline{X}_1^* = \frac{1}{K}\sum_{i=1}^{K} X_i^* \qquad \overline{X}_2^* = \frac{1}{K}\sum_{i=K+1}^{n} X_i^*.$$

The estimates of a and b are

$$\hat{b} = \frac{\overline{Y}_1^* - \overline{Y}_2^*}{\overline{X}_1^* - \overline{X}_2^*} \qquad (5\text{-}39)$$

and

$$\hat{a} = \overline{Y}^* - \hat{b}\overline{X}^*. \qquad (5\text{-}40)$$

[†]Wald, "The Fitting of Straight Lines If Both Variables Are Subject to Error," *Annual of Mathematical Statistics*, Vol. 11 (1940), pp. 284–300.

These estimates are consistent. However, when the variables are normally distributed, the results are no longer consistent estimates, as shown by Wald.

3. There is another method of correction that makes use of maximum-likelihood estimation. This method estimates the error variances of the dependent and independent variables. The estimation method is shown by Johnston.†

5.5   Lagged Variables

5.5.1   Causes and Effects

The lagged variable refers to the time-lagged values of the dependent variable or independent variable in the regression model. Lagged variables have been adopted to a great extent in recent econometric work, based on an assumption that the dependent variable responds to the past value of the dependent variable or to the response to the independent variable with a delay. An example follows:

Consider the equations

$$C_t = a + bY_t + cC_{t-1} + U_t \qquad (5\text{-}41)$$

and

$$C_t = a + bY_{t-1} + U_t', \qquad (5\text{-}42)$$

where C_t and C_{t-1} are consumptions in periods t and $t - 1$, respectively, and Y_t and Y_{t-1} are incomes in periods t and $t - 1$, respectively. Equation (5-41) implies that current consumption depends not only on the current income but also on past consumption. Past consumption is included for the habit-persistence assumption. Equation (5-42) makes a similar assumption, but the lagged income is used instead of current income and lagged consumption.

Applying the least-squares estimation to Equation (5-42) presents no problem, since Y_{t-1} is uncorrelated with U_t. However, for Equation (5-41) the classical least-squares estimation produces biased results. Consider a simple form

$$C_t = a + bC_{t-1} + U_t, \qquad (5\text{-}43)$$

†Johnston, *Econometric Methods* (New York, McGraw-Hill, 1963).

assuming that U_t are independently distributed with mean 0 and variance σ^2. The least-squares estimate of b is

$$\hat{b} = \frac{\sum\limits_{t=2}^{n} (C_t - \overline{C})(C_{t-1} - \widetilde{C})}{\sum\limits_{t=2}^{n} (C_{t-1} - \widetilde{C})^2}, \qquad (5\text{-}44)$$

where $C = [1/(n-1)](C_2 + C_3 + \cdots + C_n)$ and $\widetilde{C} = [1/(n-1)](C_1 + C_2 + \cdots + C_{n-1})$. When we take the mean value of Equation (5-43), it becomes

$$\overline{C} = a + b\widetilde{C} + \overline{U}_t. \qquad (5\text{-}45)$$

Equation (5-43) minus Equation (5-45) results in

$$C_t - \overline{C}_t = b(C_{t-1} - \widetilde{C}) + (U_t - \overline{U}_t). \qquad (5\text{-}46)$$

Multiplying $(C_{t-1} - \widetilde{C})$ through Equation (5-46), taking the summation and dividing through by $\Sigma(C_{t-1} - \widetilde{C})^2$, Equation (5-46) becomes

$$\hat{b} = b + \frac{\sum\limits_{t=2}^{n} (C_{t-1} - \widetilde{C})(U_t - \overline{U}_t)}{\sum\limits_{t=2}^{n} (C_t - \widetilde{C})^2}$$

$$= b + \frac{\sum\limits_{t=2}^{n} (C_{t-1} - \widetilde{C})U_t}{\sum\limits_{t=2}^{n} (C_t - \widetilde{C})^2} \qquad \text{since } \sum\limits_{t=2}^{n} (C_{t-1} - \widetilde{C})\overline{U}_t = 0.$$

$$(5\text{-}47)$$

The expectation of

$$\sum\limits_{t=2}^{n} (C_{t-1} - \widetilde{C})U_t = \sum\limits_{t=2}^{n} EC_{t-1} U_t - \sum\limits_{t=2}^{n} E\widetilde{C}\, U_t$$

$$= - \sum\limits_{t=2}^{n} E\widetilde{C}\, U_t$$

$$\neq 0,$$

since U_t are correlated with $\widetilde{C}$; that is, $C_1, C_2, \ldots, C_{t-1}$. Therefore, the classical least-squares estimate of b is biased.

91

Problems in Single-Equation Regression Estimation

The lagged variable has been extended further by Koyck,[†] Cagan,[‡] and Nerlove.[§] Nerlove's model introduced the expectation and adjustment models in the econometric analysis. A brief summary is presented.

The expectation model suggests that the variable Y_t is determined by the expected value of X_t, X_t^*. Several examples can be illustrated in terms of this concept: the current consumption is a function of the expected income; or the supply of a given commodity is a function of the expected price of the commodity. Suppose that

$$Y_t = a + bX_t^* + U_t , \qquad (5\text{-}48)$$

where U_t is independently distributed with 0 mean and variance σ^2. Further, we assume that expectations are formed recursively as follows:

$$X_t^* = X_{t-1}^* + c(X_t - X_{t-1}^*) \qquad 0 < c < 1, \qquad (5\text{-}49)$$

where c is the *coefficient of expectation*. Substituting Equation (5-49) into Equation (5-48) and rearranging, we get

$$Y_t = ac + bc\, X_t + (1 - c)\, Y_{t-1} + [U_t - (1 - c)\, U_{t-1}]. \qquad (5\text{-}50)$$

In this model, although we have specified the explicit form of the expectation, we have introduced a statistical problem. That is, Y_{t-1} is correlated with a part of the error term $U_t - (1 - c)U_{t-1}$; that is, U_{t-1}. Therefore, the classical least-squares estimation is not appropriate. Furthermore, the error term $U_t - (1 - c)U_{t-1}$ is no longer serially independent.

$$E[U_t - (1 - c)U_{t-1} - (1 - c)U_{t-2}] = -(1 - c)\sigma^2$$

$$= (c - 1)\sigma^2$$

$$\neq 0 \qquad (5\text{-}51)$$

[†]Koyck, *Distributed Lags and Investment Analysis* (Amsterdam, North-Holland, 1954).

[‡]Cagan, "The Monetary Dynamics of Hyperinflation," in *Studies in the Quantity Theory of Money*, Milton Fiedman, ed. (Chicago, University of Chicago Press, 1956).

[§]Nerlove, *Distributed Lags and Demand Analysis for Agricultural and Other Commodities* (Washington, U.S. Department of Agriculture, 1958).

The adjustment model assumes that the desired value of Y_t, Y_t^*, is a function of X_t. An economic example would be that the desired amount of cash balance is a function of an individual's income. Suppose that

$$Y_t^* = a + bX_t + U_t, \qquad (5\text{-}52)$$

where U_t is independently distributed with 0 mean and variance σ^2. Furthermore, we assume that the adjustment to the desired value in one period is

$$Y_t = Y_{t-1} + d\,(Y_t^* - Y_{t-1}) \qquad 0 < d < 1, \qquad (5\text{-}53)$$

where d is the *coefficient of adjustment*. Inserting Equation (5-52) into Equation (5-53), and rewriting gives

$$Y_t = ad + bdX_t + (1 - d)\,Y_{t-1} + dU_t. \qquad (5\text{-}54)$$

Equation (5-54) presents the same estimation problem as does Equation (5-50). Therefore, classical least-squares estimation of Equation (5-54) will result in biased estimates.

It is possible to have both expectation and adjustment lags in the same model. Then the equation can be written

$$Y_t^* = a + bX_t^* + U_t, \qquad (5\text{-}55)$$

where U_t is independently distributed with 0 mean and variance σ^2. Substituting Equation (5-55) into Equation (5-53), and then making successive substitutions from Equation (5-49) for X_t^*, we get

$$Y_t = acd + bcd\,X_t + [(1 - c) + (1 - d)]\,Y_{t-1}$$
$$- (1 - c)\,(1 - d)\,Y_{t-2} + d[U_t - (1 - d)\,U_{t-1}\,]. $$
$$(5\text{-}56)$$

Equation (5-56) is a general form for either the expectation model or the adjustment model. The solutions of c and d are symmetrical. When $d = 1$, then Equation (5-56) becomes the expectation model; when $c = 1$, then Equation (5-56) becomes the adjustment model. If either c or d equals 1, then the estimated regression coefficient associated with Y_{t-2} will not be statistically significant. Again error terms in Equation (5-56) are serially correlated.

5.5.2 Estimation Methods

The effects of lagged dependent variables in the regression model result in a serial correlation of the error term and correlation between the lagged dependent variable and the error terms; thus, the classical least-squares estimates are biased. Several alternative methods can overcome these problems.

1. Cagan† estimated Equation (5-48) by reformulating Equation (5-49). Since Equation (5-49) implies that the X_t^* can be constructed as exponentially weighted averages of X_t and past values of X_t, where the parameter c is a geometrically declining distributed lag,

$$X_t^* = \sum_{i=0}^{\infty} c(1 - c)^i X_{t-i}. \qquad (5\text{-}57)$$

Cagan used such a variable by trying out different c's, constructing the associated $\hat{X}_t^*$ series, and choosing that c that led to the highest R^2 in Equation (5-48). In fact, the resulting estimates are maximum-likelihood estimates, provided the model is correct.

But when this method is applied to Equation (5-55), difficulties arise in discriminating the coefficient of expectation c from the coefficient of adjustment d, since the solutions of c and d are symmetrical.

2. In order to deal with the problems of autocorrelated error terms, as suggested by Fuller and Martin,‡ we define $U_t - (1 - c)U_{t-1} = V_t$ and assume that

$$V_t = \rho V_{t-1} + e_t \qquad -1 \leqslant \rho < 1, \qquad (5\text{-}58)$$

where ρ is the autoregressive coefficient and e_t is a nonautocorrelated error term with 0 mean. By solving Equation (5-50) for V_t, lagging each variable one time period, and substituting into Equation (5-58), we get

$$Y_t = ac(1 - \rho) + bcX_t - bc\rho X_{t-1} + [(1 - c) + \rho]Y_{t-1}$$
$$- (1 - c)\rho \, Y_{t-2} + e_t. \qquad (5\text{-}59)$$

There are five regression coefficients in Equation (5-59), but it contains only four original parameters, a, b, c, and ρ. Therefore, no unique solution exists for a, b, c, and ρ. A constrained nonlinear

†Cagan, op. cit.
‡Fuller and Martin, "The Effects of Autocorrelated Errors in the Statistical Estimation of Distributed Lag Models," *Journal of Farm Economics*, Vol. 41 (1961), pp. 81–82.

least-squares estimation is required to obtain unique estimates of these four parameters. The nonlinear least-squares estimation is discussed by Draper and Smith.†

The other source of bias is that Y_{t-1} and Y_{t-2} may be correlated with V_t. To overcome this problem we use a two-stage procedure, substituting for Y_{t-1} and Y_{t-2} by means of least-squares to estimate $\hat{Y}_{t-1}$ and $\hat{Y}_{t-2}$ as a function of lagged X_t, as suggested by Griliches.‡

3. Two other approaches may solve the lagged dependent variable problems. One is by Koyck. However, this method of correction is quite cumbersome. The detailed estimation procedure is shown by Goldberger.§ One other correction method is suggested by Klein.¶ Klein's method is that if we assume that the error terms in Equation (5-50) are nonautocorrelated and not derived from Equation (5-48), then the classical least-squares estimation is permitted.

†Draper and Smith, *Applied Regression Analysis* (New York, Wiley, 1968).
‡Griliches, "Distributed Lags: A Survey," *Econometrica*, Vol. 35 (1967), pp. 16–49.
§ Goldberger, *op. cit.*
¶ Klein, "The Estimation of Distributed Lags," *Econometrica*, Vol. 26 (October 1958), pp. 553–565.

6

APPLICATIONS OF THE SINGLE-EQUATION REGRESSION MODEL

6.1 Nature of Data

6.1.1 Time-Series Versus Cross-Section Data

Sample observations collected by most econometric studies can be classified into three categories: time-series data, cross-section data, and the combined time-series and cross-section data.

Time-series data are obtained at many points of time, such as monthly, quarterly, or annually for the same economic unit—household, firm, industry, or country. For example, a consumption function is estimated from annual consumption against annual income for a given time-series. Econometricians usually gather a time-series sample to study specific economic behavior. However, since systematic government data collection and publication were launched in the early 1930s, the sample size of most time-series data is rather limited. Furthermore, within the time period the samples are nonuniform in the sense that there are war years or depression periods that may belong to a different universe.

Another type of sample commonly used is obtained from cross-section data. Cross-section data refer to activities of an individual economic unit, such as family, firms, industries, states, or countries for a given time period. A family-expenditure survey is an example. The sample size of a cross-section data is not as limited as is that of a time-series data. For instance, in a sample survey, with some financial effort, one can easily expand a sample size from 100 to 1000 sample units.

Because of the different nature of these two kinds of data, empirical analysis based on them may result in different economic implications. The point can be best illustrated with an example of a demand study. In cross-section analysis, estimation of demand is based on budget data. The variations in income among the households in the cross-section income data are much larger than the variations in time-series income data as observed from aggregate households. Most consumers' income levels are fairly stable over time. In other words, for a group of families covered by the family-budget data, the changes in income that occur in the course of time are, on the whole, small and infrequent, as compared with the existing income differences between the families in the group. The basic assumption in cross-section analysis is that a relatively poor family would consume as much of a certain commodity as a relatively rich family if its income were to become as large as that of the relatively rich family. However, there may be a time lag in the adoption of new consumption habits as income rises. Thus, it is only in the long-run that the upward income changes of a relatively poor family might result in a consumption pattern similar to that of the relatively rich family. Accordingly, the results of time-series analysis may be designated as short-run, and the results of cross-section analysis as long-run. In other words, in the analysis of cross-section data different consumers are assumed homogeneous, whereas in the analysis of time-series data the different periods of time are assumed homogeneous.

Some econometric studies combine both time-series and cross-section data. There are two approaches to pooling time-series and cross-section data. One is to make use of cross-section information in order to obtain the parameters of the regression model and then to transform these estimated parameters into a new equation to be estimated from time-series data, such as the example discussed in Section 5.1.2. The incorporation of the cross-section data into time-series analysis will make full use of information from both time-series and cross-section data to estimate the regression model. For example, for a demand function, income elasticity can be estimated from cross-section data associated with income, family size, and residence, while prices are held constant. Given the estimated income elasticity, time-series market data can be used to estimate the demand parameters associated with prices. Another advantage in using the pooling method is that the problem of multicollinearity among the independent variables can be remedied. One common phenomenon in time-series data is the multicollinearity between income and prices, as we discussed in Section 5.1.

The second approach to pooling time-series and cross-section data is to combine the sample observations for the same economic unit over several time periods. This method, of course, is richer in data than either time-series or cross-section data alone. Furthermore, for a given period cross-section data the observed value for economic units may appear to be "transitory" in nature, but a group of observations for the same economic unit over a given time period may reduce the possible fluctuation or transitory phenomenon. A statistical problem may arise from the combination of cross-section and time-series data. One may argue that the cross-section sample may represent a different population from the time-series sample. In other words, the error variance of cross-section data may be different from the error variance of time-series data. Therefore, the classical least-squares method may not be appropriate to estimate the parameters of the pooled data.

If one is not primarily interested in acquiring a larger sample size by combining cross-section and time-series data but if he wishes rather to avoid the transitory short-run factors that may occur in any given year's cross-section data, then he can take the average value of each cross-section observation over several time periods, say, four or five years. This method will average out the transitory effects.

6.1.2 Aggregation Problem

Most time-series or cross-section data, except the household-survey data, are aggregate in nature, in the sense that the reporting economic unit is either in terms of a national, state, or industry unit. However, economic theories are mostly derived from analysis based on the individual's or a single firm's behavior. Therefore, the results from aggregate data do not exactly depict the results of a single individual's or firm's behavior. For example, the economic theory of consumer behavior is formulated for an individual's demand function. However, the demand functions considered in most demand studies are based on market data—national totals or averages. This suggests the following question: What is the relation between the estimated market-demand parameters and the individual parameters? This question comprises the aggregation problem.

We will use a typical demand function to explain the aggregation problem. In demand studies two types of aggregation exist: one with respect to the aggregation of individual consumer behavior and the other with respect to aggregation of commodities or services. In order to simplify the presentation of these aggregation problems a linear individual demand function is assumed. Suppose that the jth individual's demand for the ith commodity can be expressed as

$$q_{ij} = a_{0\,ij} + a_{1\,ij}\,p_{1j} + a_{2\,ij}\,p_{2j} + \cdots + a_{n\,ij}\,p_{nj}$$
$$+ b_{ij}\,y_j + u_{ij} \qquad j = 1, 2, \ldots, H. \qquad (6\text{-}1)$$

The time subscript is omitted for convenience. Quantities demanded (q_i), prices ($p_1, p_2, \ldots, p_n$), incomes (y), and disturbances (u_{ij}) are assumed to vary among individuals. Market demand is obtained by aggregating over individual demand:

$$\sum_{j=1}^{H} q_{ij} = \sum_{j=1}^{H} a_{0\,ij} + \sum_{j=1}^{H} a_{1\,ij}p_{1j} + \sum_{j=1}^{H} a_{2\,ij}p_{2j} + \cdots$$

$$+ \sum_{j=1}^{H} a_{n\,ij}p_{nj} + \sum_{j=1}^{H} b_{1\,j}y_j + \sum_{j=1}^{H} u_{1j}. \qquad (6\text{-}2)$$

Equation (6-2) may also be written on an average or per capita basis:

$$Q_i = A_{0\,i} + A_{1\,i}P_1 + A_{2\,i}P_2 + \cdots + A_{n\,i}P_n + B_iY + U_i, \qquad (6\text{-}3)$$

where Q_i denotes per capita consumption of the ith good, $P_1, P_2, \ldots, P_n$ denote average prices of $q_1, q_2, \ldots,$ Y denotes per capita disposable income, and

$$A_{0\,i} = \frac{1}{H}\sum_{j=1}^{H} a_{0\,ij}, \qquad (6\text{-}4)$$

$$A_{k\,i} = \sum_{j=1}^{H} a_{k\,ij}p_{kj} \bigg/ \sum_{j=1}^{H} p_{kj} \qquad k = 1, 2, \ldots, n, \qquad (6\text{-}5)$$

$$B_i = \sum_{j=1}^{H} b_{ij}y_j \bigg/ \sum_{j=1}^{H} y_j \qquad (6\text{-}6)$$

$$U_i = \frac{1}{H}\sum_{j=1}^{H} u_{ij}. \qquad (6\text{-}7)$$

The coefficients of A_{ki} and B_i are weighted arithmetic means of the individual a_{ki} and b_i, the weights being the individual $p_1, p_2, \ldots, p_n$ and y, respectively. Coefficients in Equation (6-3) will be constant; that is, independent of time, under the following conditions: (1) the distribution of prices and incomes does not change over the time period considered or (2) all prices change in fixed proportion K_p and all incomes change in fixed proportion K_y, or (3) the correlations between a_{kij} and p_{kj} and b_{ij} and y_j, respectively, are 0 at all time periods. For case (3) the parameters A_{ki} and B_i are simple averages of the individual a_{kij} and b_{ij}. Case (1), (2), or (3) is usually assumed when a linear aggregate demand function is fitted statistically to average prices, per capita consumption, and income data over a period of years. Detailed discussions are shown in Fox.[†]

The subject of commodities also presents problems of aggregation. For example, dairy products are composed of various types of fluid milk, butter, or cheese. Normally, aggregation over individual commodities and aggregation over individual consumers are equivalent processes, as shown in Allen.[‡] In the case of dairy products the aggregate quantity (fluid milk equivalent) is defined as a weighted sum of all individual dairy products. The standard weights are calculated by the Department of Agriculture according to the *fat solid basis* of individual dairy products.

6.2 Demand Function

6.2.1 Theoretical Formulation

The first step in carrying out an econometric study is to formulate a model based on economic theory. This section demonstrates how to make use of economic theory by means of mathematical tools to formulate a quantifiable econometric model.

The consumer's demand curve for a given commodity can be derived from the analysis of utility maximization.

[†]Fox, *Econometric Analysis for Public Policy* (Ames, Iowa, State University Press, 1958).

[‡]Allen, *Mathematical Economics* (New York, Macmillan, 1956), pp. 694–724.

The classical theory of consumer behavior begins with a utility function that makes an individual's level of satisfaction depend on the commodities he consumes.

Let a consumer's ordinal utility function be

$$u = f(q_1, q_2, \ldots, q_n), \tag{6-8}$$

where $q_1, q_2, \ldots, q_n$ are the quantities of the different commodities consumed in a single time period. It is assumed that the utility function in Equation (6-8) is not only an increasing and continuous function of each of the quantities but is also twice differentiable.

Given the utility function in Equation (6-8), the theory assumes that consumer behavior is explicable by maximization of Equation (6-8) with respect to the q's subject to a budget constraint; namely,

$$\sum_{i=1}^{n} p_i q_i = y. \tag{6-9}$$

The prices $p_1, p_2, \ldots, p_n$ and income y are taken as given to the consumer, and they satisfy the following conditions:

$$p_i > 0 \qquad i = 1, 2, \ldots, n \text{ and } y > 0. \tag{6-10}$$

The maximization of Equation (6-8) subject to Equation (6-9) is a constrained maximum problem. A necessary condition for the solution of this type of problem is that

$$u_i - \lambda p_i = 0 \qquad i = 1, 2, \ldots, n. \tag{6-11}$$

where $u_i = (\partial u / \partial q_i)$ and λ is the Lagrange multiplier. In economic term, λ is the marginal utility of money. From this it follows that

$$\frac{u_i}{u_j} = \frac{p_i}{p_j} \qquad i, j = 1, 2, \ldots, n. \tag{6-12}$$

and also that

$$\frac{u_i}{p_i} = \lambda \qquad i = 1, 2, \ldots, n. \tag{6-13}$$

Thus, in equilibrium the ratio of the marginal utilities of two commodities is equal to the ratio of their prices; that is, the marginal utilities are proportional to the prices.

Equations (6-9) and (6-11) provide $(1+n)$ relationships that permit the $(1 + n)$ unknowns, λ and q_i $(i = 1, \ldots, n)$,

101

to be expressed in terms of y and p_i $(i = 1, \ldots, n)$. Thus the solution yields the following demand functions:

$$q_i = f_i\,(p_1, p_2, \ldots, p_n, y) \qquad i = 1, 2, \ldots, n. \tag{6-14}$$

In other words, Equation (6-14) states that consumer demand for the ith good depends on income and the prices of all commodities.

It should be noted that equal proportionate changes in prices and income do not affect the constraint in Equation (6-9) and thus will not affect the utility maximizing values of the q's. Adopting this property of zero-degree homogeneity, Equation (6-14) can be written as

$$q_i = f_i\left(\frac{p_1}{p}, \frac{p_2}{p}, \ldots, \frac{p_n}{p}, \frac{y}{p}\right) \qquad i = 1, 2, \ldots, n, \tag{6-15}$$

where p is an index of general prices. Equation (6-15) states that the demand for q_i is a function of relative prices of all commodities and real income.

In addition to prices and income, other factors, such as tastes, determine consumer demand. The factors determining preferences such as family size and composition and residential area, may be noted by x_j, where $j = 1, 2, \ldots, m$. Thus, the demand relationship for an individual consumer may be written in the form

$$q_i = f_i\left(\frac{p_1}{p}, \frac{p_2}{p}, \ldots, \frac{p_n}{p}, \frac{y}{p}, x_1, x_2, \ldots, x_m\right)$$

$$i = 1, 2, \ldots n. \tag{6-16}$$

Since the utility function is not measurable in practice, statistical analysis begins directly with the demand functions. The exact functional form is rarely deduced theoretically but is usually determined empirically.

Equation (6-16) is a general function for empirical estimation of a demand analysis. However, there are several reasons that, in practice, a regression is not specified in a study so as to include all factors that may have causal influence on the dependent variable under analysis. First, it is legitimate to make the demand theory as simple as possible, taking into explicit account only the main causal factors. Second, statistical data are lacking for certain variables. Finally, the causal factors may be highly intercorrelated. Inclusion of a large number of explanatory variables in the model may increase the standard errors of the regression coefficients and tend to obscure the importance of explanatory variables in the equation.

Finally, before we estimate a demand function empirically, we face an identification problem. Namely, how do we know that the specified function is not, rather, a supply curve? In other words, how can we distinguish the demand function from the supply function? In fact, the collected economic data are already in equilibrium condition where supply is equal to demand. This identification problem is discussed in detail in Chapter 7.

6.2.2 Empirical Examples

The pioneer study in demand analysis was done by Schulz.† He estimated statistically the demand functions for wheat, sugar, corn, cotton, and other agricultural commodities. In the Schultz study the problems of identification, multicollinearity, and autocorrelation were not explored.

We choose two studies as empirical examples of demand analysis. Both examples estimated the demand for automobiles in the United States. One is estimated by Stone in his comprehensive work on demand analysis in the United States and the United Kingdom.‡

His fundamental equation takes the form

$$q = a\, Q^b p^c \pi^d e^{rt}, \tag{6-17}$$

where

q = the quantity of the automobile demanded per year
Q = real disposable income per year
p = the annual average price of the automobile
π = the annual average price of all other commodities
t = time in years
e = the base of natural logarithms.

Stone used annual time-series data from 1929 to 1941 to estimate Equation (6-17). He tried a number of alternative

---

†Schultz, *The Theory and Measurement of Demand* (Chicago, The University of Chicago Press, 1938).
‡Stone, "The Analysis of Market Demand," *Journal of Royal Statistical Society*, Vol. 108 (1945), pp. 286–382.

specifications of the model, but he concluded that the following is the most desirable estimation:

$$q = 1.2103 \ Q^{4.164} \ p^{-2.704} \ e^{0.067t}. \qquad (6\text{-}18)$$

We pointed out in Section 4.1 that Equation (6-18) can be expressed in a linear doublelog form. Furthermore, each coefficient in Equation (6-18) is the elasticity of the demand for automobiles with respect to each independent variable. These elasticities are constant elasticities. Equation (6-18) indicates that the income elasticity of the demand for automobiles is 4.16 and that the price elasticity of the demand for automobiles is -2.70. Therefore, Stone suggested that the demand for automobiles is highly sensitive to income and automobile prices.

The second example of demand analysis is a study done by Suits.† He studied the demand for new automobiles in the United States from 1929 to 1956. The final formulation of the demand function, annual retail sales of new passenger automobile (R) are explained by:

1. real disposable income (Y);
2. stock of passenger cars at the beginning of the year (S);
3. the average real retail price of new passenger cars divided by the average number of month's duration of automobile credit contracts P/M. Thus, this price variable is an index of monthly payment associated with the purchase of passenger cars; and
4. A dummy variable to take account of the special conditions of the automobile market in years of severe production shortage (X).

Over the period under analysis, the war years from 1942 to 1945 and the following years from 1946 to 1948 were omitted from the sample because of the existence of a possible disequilibrium. Like most time-series data, there may be an autocorrelation existing in the error terms. To avoid this problem all variables are measured in terms of first differences. This application may also reduce the relative effect of such slowly changing factors as consumer tastes or population, thus giving a better estimation of the effect of the factors included in the equation. The dummy variable is defined as 1 in 1941 and 1952; -1 in 1953; and

†Suits, "The Demand for New Automobiles in the United States 1929–1956," *Review of Economics and Statistics* (August 1958), pp. 273–281.

0 in all other years.   The equation is estimated by least squares:

$$\Delta R = 0.115 + 0.106\,\Delta Y - 0.507\,\Delta S - 0.234\Delta\,(P/M)$$
$$\quad\quad (0.011)\quad\quad (0.086)\quad\quad (0.088)$$

$$\quad - 0.827\,\Delta X$$
$$\quad\ \ (0.261)$$

$$\overline{R}^2 = 0.85. \tag{6-19}$$

Figures in parentheses are standard errors of the regression coefficients. $\overline{R}^2$ is the adjusted coefficient of determination. R and S are measured in millions of cars; Y is in billions of dollars from 1947 to 1949; P/M is an index.   All regression coefficients are statistically significant from 0 at the 1% level.

Based on the regression coefficients in Equation (6-19), Suits calculated the elasticities of demand for new cars based on the sample means. The method of computing elasticity from a linear-regression model is shown in Section 4.1.   In this case X and Y are evaluated at $\overline{X}$ and $\overline{Y}$.   Suits' estimates of the elasticity of the demand for a new car with respect to real disposable income is 4.16, the elasticity of the demand for new cars with respect to the stock of cars is - 3.65, and the elasticity of the demand for new cars with respect to the index of real monthly payment is - 0.58.   Surprisingly enough, Suits' estimates on income elasticity are almost identical to Stone's estimates, although each used a different time period of data and a different functional form.

Suits experimented with including the rate of increase in income in his model, but this variable was not statistically significant.   Another way to examine the acceleration effect of the demand for the new cars is to formulate a dynamic model. That is, Suits suggested the formulation of a new variable to express the expected rate of change from actual income to desired level of income. However, he did not provide the empirical estimation of this dynamic model.

6.3   Production Function

6.3.1   Theoretical Formulation

A production function is a technical relation showing how inputs are transformed into outputs.   The inputs are considered as land, labor, and capital. In econometric analysis we often use man-hours as the measurement for labor, machine-hours as the measurement for capital, and land-depletion as the measurement for land. Output is defined as the finished products that are measured as a flow of goods and services during a given time period. The production function is

$$Q = f(X_1, X_2, \ldots, X_n), \qquad (6\text{-}20)$$

where Q is the maximum amount of output that a firm can produce for given amount of inputs $X_1, X_2, \ldots, X_n$, such as land, labor, and capital. Unlike the demand function the production function can be derived from the above proposition. Indeed, the existence of such a function already presupposes an optimum combination of inputs in the firm's behavior. The variables and parameters of the production function are independent of market prices of inputs and outputs. One may relate this formulation in a fashion similar to the utility function in the demand analysis.

The data used in the estimation of a production function can be either a time-series or a cross-section sample. Time-series data may contain a series of observations for outputs and inputs for a given firm or a given industry over a period. It is often argued that the state of technology is another important factor affecting the level of output. Over a period of time technology may improve. In order to take account of technical change, one may include a time-trend variable in the production function as a proxy for measurement of technological change.

$$Q_t = f(X_{1t}, X_{2t}, \ldots, X_{nt}, t). \qquad (6\text{-}21)$$

Cross-section data can be obtained from individual firms or industries in a given period. The most common way is to collect output and input data from firms within an industry.

One important problem in the empirical analysis of a production function is to determine what happens to output when all inputs are increased proportionately. This situation comprises the returns to scale problem. There is some empirical evidence that production functions for the economy as a whole approximate constant returns to scale. This particular function is called a linear homogeneous production function. The analysis of this particular form was summarized by Douglas.† Douglas and Cobb presented their production function as

$$Q = A \, L^\alpha C^\beta, \qquad (6\text{-}22)$$

where

Q = output
L = labor input
C = capital input.

The sum of the exponents in Equation (6-22) shows the degree of returns to scale in production.

$\alpha + \beta < 1$ decreasing returns to scale
$\alpha + \beta = 1$ constant returns to scale
$\alpha + \beta > 1$ increasing returns to scale.

As we explained in Section 4.1, each parameter in Equation (6-22) is also the constant elasticity of output with respect to its input.

In the past decade, since Arrow and others‡ introduced the constant elasticity of substitution (*CES*) production function, there has been considerable theoretical and empirical work on the *CES* production function. As Arrow and coworkers have shown, the Cobb–Douglas production is only a special case of *CES* production function with elasticity of substitution equal to 1.

6.3.2 Empirical Examples

Two examples of production functions are illustrated. We first choose the pioneer study by Cobb and Douglas §, whose original formulation of the production function is

$$p = b \, L^k \, C^{1-k} \, U, \qquad (6\text{-}23)$$

where P is an index of total production per year, L is an index of labor inputs, C is an index of capital inputs, and U is an error term. The sample indexes were from 1899 to 1922, based on 1899 = 100. They argue that b is indepen-

---

†Douglas, "Are There Laws of Production?" *American Economic Review*, Vol. 38 (1948), pp. 1–41.

‡Arrow and others, "Capital-Labor Substitution and Economic Efficiency," *The Review of Economics and Statistics* (August 1961), pp. 225–250.

§Cobb and Douglas, "A Theory of Production," *American Economic Review*, Vol. 18 (May 1928), pp. 139–165.

dent of L and C. The coefficient b is supposed to catch all those quantitative effects of any force for which they did not have quantitative data. The least-squares technique was used to estimate the model. The results are

$$P = 1.01 \ L^{3/4} \ C^{1/4} . \tag{6-24}$$

No R^2 and standard errors of the coefficient were provided in the study. Equation (6-24) indicates that for a 1% increase in labor input with the amount of capital held constant, total output will increase by $\frac{3}{4}$ of 1%. On the other hand, with a 1% increase in capital input and the amount of labor held constant, the total output will increase by $\frac{1}{4}$ of 1%. On the whole, if both labor and capital increase by 1%, the total output will increase by 1%. It is in this sense that this production function has the property of constant returns to scale.

The second empirical example is drawn from a recent study of Feldstein, an analysis of health-service efficiency in the United Kingdom.† In his study Feldstein used the Cobb–Douglas production function to examine the returns to scale in the health-service industry. Here output is defined as the total number of cases in a given hospital. However, the cases treated are nonhomogeneous. A linear aggregation of the number of cases treated is not a meaningful technique for aggregating hospital services. Therefore, Feldstein used a measure of weighted output (W), which is defined as the sum of relative average costs with respect to each case treated. Hospital inputs include doctors (M), beds (B), nurses (N), and other supplies (S). Again, doctors and nurses vary in quality and seniority so that instead of aggregating them by number of hours worked, Feldstein measured them by total staff expenditures for doctors and nurses, respectively. Other supplies are also measured in expenditures. Only beds are measured in physical terms.

Based on 177 large, acute, nonteaching hospitals, during 1960 to 1961, the production function is estimated by ordinary least squares:

$$W = A \ M^{0.387}_{(0.071)} \ B^{0.465}_{(0.098)} \ N^{0.047}_{(0.096)} \ S^{0.069}_{(0.111)} \qquad R^2 = 0.90, \tag{6-25}$$

†Feldstein, *Economic Analysis of Health Service Efficiency* (Amsterdam, North-Holland, 1967).

where A is a constant term, the value of which is not reported. Values in parentheses are the standard error of the coefficient.

The sum of these coefficients is equal to 0.968, which implies that hospitals, on the average, experience constant returns to scale. The standard error of the sum of these coefficients is 0.026. The calculation formula is

$$[V(\alpha_M) + V(\alpha_B) + V(\alpha_N) + V(\alpha_S) + 2\text{cov}(\alpha_M \alpha_B)$$
$$+ 2\text{cov}(\alpha_M \alpha_N) + 2\text{cov}(\alpha_M \alpha_S) + 2\text{cov}(\alpha_B \alpha_N)$$
$$+ 2(\alpha_B \alpha_S) + 2(\alpha_N \alpha_S)]^{1/2}.$$

6.4 Cost Function

6.4.1 Theoretical Formulation

The simplest form for a cost function is a bivariate relation between total cost and levels of output. The theory of the firm assumes that a firm attempts to minimize its total cost for a given level of output. The total cost function can be derived from a production function under the assumption that a firm attempts to minimize its total cost for a given level of output.

Let a firm's total cost be

$$C = P_1 X_1 + P_2 X_2 + \cdots + P_n X_n, \qquad (6\text{-}26)$$

where $X_1, X_2, \ldots, X_n$ are the quantities of the different inputs used to produce output Q. $P_1, P_2, \ldots, P_n$ are the respective input prices for $X_1, X_2, \ldots, X_n$. The theory assumes that if a firm is to minimize its costs subject to its production constraint, a given level Q:

$$Q = f(X_1, X_2, \ldots, X_n). \qquad (6\text{-}27)$$

To obtain the Lagrange expression for this constrained minimization problem, a necessary condition for the solution of this problem is that

$$P_i - \lambda x_i = 0 \qquad i = 1, 2, \ldots, n. \qquad (6\text{-}28)$$

where $x_i = (\partial Q/\partial X_i)$ and λ is the Langrange multiplier. From this it follows that

$$\frac{P_i}{P_j} = \frac{x_i}{x_j} \qquad i,j = 1, 2, \ldots, n \qquad (6.29)$$

109

and also that

$$\frac{x_i}{P_i} = \lambda \qquad i, j, = 1, 2, \ldots, n. \qquad (6\text{-}30)$$

Thus, in equilibrium, the ratio of marginal productivity of two inputs is equal to the ratio of their prices; that is, the marginal productivities are proportional to the prices.

Equations (6-27) and (6-28) provide $(1 + n)$ relationships, which permit $(1 + n)$ unknowns, λ and $X_i (i = 1, 2, \ldots, n)$ to be expressed in terms of a given Q, Q^*, and $p_i (1, 2, \ldots, n)$. Thus, the solution yields the following demand for inputs function:

$$X_i = f_i(P_1, P_2, \ldots, P_n, Q^*). \qquad (6\text{-}31)$$

If we multiply each X_i by its price P_i and take the summation, we get

$$\sum P_i X_i = \sum P_i f_i(P_1, P_2, \ldots, P_n, Q^*)$$

or

$$C = f(P_1, P_2, \ldots, P_n, Q^*). \qquad (6\text{-}32)$$

Equation (6-32) is the total cost function, derived from the production function under the assumption of cost minimization. Equation (6-32) implies that the cost function depends on input prices as well as on total outputs.

In most empirical cost-function studies variables for input prices are not included in the model. The theoretical argument for this omission is that if the market is competitive, then the price of any given input is equal for all firms; therefore, the input-price variables can be deleted. In some cases input-price variables are desirable but no data are available. Thus, the omission of the price variable occurs regardless.

There is a theoretical distinction between the short-run cost function and the long-run cost function. The short-run cost function assumes that the size of plant is fixed. However, in the long-run cost function all costs can be varied so that the size of a plant can be varied. A convenient way of distinguishing the empirical cost-function estimation between short-run and long-run is by the differences in data used in their estimation. For a short-run cost function one includes only the operating costs, such as the costs of material and costs of labor in the cost-function estimation. On the other hand, depreciation costs and other nonoperating costs should be included in the long-run cost-function estimation.

There is another way of differentiating the long-run and short-run cost function. Johnston suggested that in the long run the plant size varies.† Therefore, one can include the variable of plant size in the cost function, which can be considered long run in nature. The cost function that does not contain the plant size variable can be considered short run in nature.

6.4.2 Empirical Examples

We choose two empirical cost functions as examples. One is Dean's work on the cost function of a hosiery mill.‡ The other is Johnston's work on a cost function of electricity plants in the United Kingdom.§

Dean used monthly data of operating costs of a silk-hosiery mill during the period 1935 to 1939. The size of the plant was not changed during the period. Based on these data he estimated the short-run cost function for this mill. His first simple linear-regression line between costs and output shows that it has a very good fit.

$$X_1 = 2935.59 + 1.998X_2 \qquad R = 0.973 \qquad (6\text{-}33)$$

where X_1 is total costs in dollars and X_2 is output in dozens of pairs. He then found that total costs are also correlated with time-trend and time-trend squared. His total cost function ends up in the following form:

$$X_1 = 13634.83 + 2.068X_2 + 1308.039X_3 - 22.280X_3{}^2,$$
$$(6\text{-}34)$$

where X_3 is the time-trend variable. Based on Equation (6-34) the marginal cost is about 2.07 dollars per dozen pairs of hose. This figure is derived from the first derivative of total cost (X_1) with respect to output (X_2); that is the regression coefficient of X_2, 2.068. Dean concludes that because his sample shows that this hosiery mill has a

†Johnston, *Statistical Cost Analysis* (New York, McGraw-Hill, 1960).
‡Dean, "Statistical Cost Functions of a Hosiery Mill," *Journal of Business of the University of Chicago*, Vol. 14, (1914), pp. 1–116.
§Johnston, *op. cit.*

linear line in this case, it provides a good approximation of the total cost function.

Dean tried a square term and a cubic term for the output variable, X_2, in the cost function. But the estimated regression coefficients of these two variables were not statistically significant from 0. Therefore, he considered Equation (6-34) to be the appropriate total cost function for the hosiery mill.

Johnston estimated cost functions of electricity-generation plants.† He divided 40 plants into two categories: 17 plants with no change of capital equipment over the sample period and 23 plants with a change in capital equipment over the sample period. Based on the first group he estimated 17 short-run cost functions, and using the second-category data he estimated 23 long-run cost functions. The sample period varies from one plant to another, ranging from 12 observations to 20 observations during the period from 1927 to 1946.

Johnston's basic function is that total cost Y is a linear function of output X. He introduced a time-trend variable T to take into account the slow changes in management techniques and production methods. However, this time variable is retained in an equation only if its coefficient is statistically different from 0. He also tried X^2 and/or X^3 in the equation. If their coefficients are statistically different from 0, then X^2 and/or X^3 are retained in the cost function.

Two of these 40 equations are illustrated here. One of his short-run cost functions is

$$Y = 3.8 + 2.439X - 0.058X^2 - 0.307T \qquad R^2 = 0.989 \;,$$
$$(0.231) \quad (0.018) \quad (0.047)$$

$$(6\text{-}35)$$

where Y is total deflated working expenses, in thousands of £, X is annual output in million units, and T is years. One of his estimated long-run cost functions is

$$Y = 9.4 + 0.591X + 0.1092X^2 - 0.240T \qquad R^2 = 0.985 \;.$$
$$(0.410) \quad (0.023) \quad (0.094)$$

$$(6\text{-}36)$$

†*Ibid.*

Marginal cost is computed by differentiating Y with respect to X. Thus, marginal cost is equal to the expression $2.439 - 2 \times 0.058X$ for Equation (6-35) and $0.591X + 2 \times 0.1092X$ for Equation (6-36). Equation (6-35) suggests that this plant has decreasing marginal cost as output increases, while Equation (6-36) indicates that the plant has increasing marginal cost. However, most of the 17 computed short-run cost functions are in linear form. Therefore, he concludes that marginal and average costs are constant over the observed range of output. However, the behavior of the long-run cost function is uncertain because of the problem of prorating capital costs over time.

6.5   Supply Function

6.5.1 Theoretical Formulation

A supply curve is a relation between the quantity of a commodity that a supplier is willing to offer at various market prices.

That is,

$$Q^* = f(P^*) , \qquad (6\text{-}37)$$

where Q^* and P^* are given. But in the process of producing the amount of a commodity, according to the theory of the firm, a supplier has to take into account his firm's production function and cost function and also consider the relation of marginal productivity to factor prices.

According to economic theory, a firm's supply curve, under the profit-maximization condition, is that portion of its marginal cost curve above the average variable cost curve, since a firm produces up to the point at which price is equal to marginal cost under the competitive market. On the other hand, the supply curve for the industry will coincide with the average cost curve.

Mathematical economics rarely derives a supply function for a commodity. The reasons perhaps lie in the discussion of the paragraph above, wherein a portion of the marginal cost curve is really a supply curve for a firm and the average cost curve is a supply curve for an industry. The other reason is that there is no supply curve in a pure monopoly case because price is set by the firm itself and

113

the firm's knowledge of its marginal cost and its marginal revenue decides the level of output.

In this section we attempt to derive a supply function based on the information of production functions and cost function. Under the assumption of cost minimization we derived the demand for inputs function from the production function as shown in Equation (6-31):

$$X_i = f_i(P_1, P_2, \ldots, P_n, Q^*).$$

If we substitute each X_i into the production function equation, (6-27), we get

$$Q = f(P_1, P_2, \ldots, P_n, Q^*). \tag{6-38}$$

Q^* is the given amount of output. When we substitute Equation (6-37) into Equation (6-38) we get

$$Q = f(P_1, P_2, \ldots, P_n, P^*), \tag{6-39}$$

where P^* is the price of the commodity Q. Equation (6-39) indicates that the supply of a commodity is a function of the input prices and of its own price.

6.5.2 Empirical Examples

In the field of empirical econometric studies, supply analysis is lacking compared to other topics such as demand, production, and costs. Most of the empirical supply studies are in the area of agricultural products. We first use Walsh's work as an example.†

Walsh assumed that the amount of cotton production is directly associated with the farmer's decision on the amount of the acreage of cotton planted. On the other hand, the decision of the acreage of cotton planted is, in turn, dependent upon last year's cotton price. Based on the annual data from 1925 to 1933, a simple regression model is estimated:

$$X_t = 32.826 + 0.918\, P_{t-1}, \tag{6-40}$$

where X_t is the acreage of cotton planted on July 1 of year t and P_{t-1} is the deflated price of cotton received by farmers in year $t - 1$. From the regression coefficient of P_{t-1}

---

†Walsh, "Response to Price in the Production of Cotton and Cottonseed," *Journal of Farm Economics*, Vol. 26 (August 1940), pp. 359–372.

Walsh estimated the elasticity of acreage with respect to last year's price to be 0.22 at the sample mean value.

The second example is Nerlove's study on the estimation of the elasticities of supply for a number of commodities.† Here we choose cotton as one of his findings. Nerlove suggested that farmers' decisions on cotton acreage are a more direct response to the expected price of cotton rather than the last year's price. One reason for the low estimates obtained by Walsh, as indicated by Nerlove, is that the elasticity of acreage is probably only a lower limit to the supply elasticity. Nerlove's hypothesis is that each year farmers revise their expected prices in proportion to the errors they made in predicting prices for the period $t - 1$. Let P_t^* be the expected price in year t, let P_{t-1}^* be the expected price in year $t - 1$, and let P_{t-1} be the actual price in year t. His formulation is

$$P_t^* - P_{t-1}^* = \beta (P_{t-1} - P_{t-1}^*), \qquad (6\text{-}41)$$

where $0 < \beta \leqslant 1$ is the coefficient of expectation. Assume that acreage response X is a function of the expected price

$$X_t = a_0 + a_1 \, p_t^* + u_t. \qquad (6\text{-}42)$$

When we substitute Equation (6-41) into Equation (6-42), the new relation becomes

$$X_t = \pi_0 + \pi_1 \, P_{t-1} + \pi_2 \, X_{t-1} + V_t, \qquad (6\text{-}43)$$

where $V_t = u_t + (1 - \beta) u_{t-1}$, $\pi_0 = a_0 \beta$, $\pi_1 = a_1 \beta$, and $\pi_2 = 1 - \beta$. From π_2 one can derive β. Then based on β, one can derive a_0 and a_1 from π_0 and π_1. Using annual data for cotton from 1909 to 1932, Nerlove obtained estimated Equation (6-43). The elasticity of acreage with respect to expected price is 0.67. This value is derived from a_1, which in turn, is obtained from π_1. The coefficient of expectation, $\beta (\beta = 1 - \pi_2)$, is 0.51, with a standard error of 0.17. Nerlove added a trend variable in the model, the coefficient of which is 0.18 with a standard error 0.12. The R^2 is 0.74. He concluded that using a price-expectation variable in the model resulted in higher elasticity of acreage with respect to price.

†Nerlove, *The Dynamics of Supply: Estimation of Farmers' Response to Price* (Baltimore, Johns Hopkins University Press, 1958).

6.6 Consumption Function

6.6.1 Theoretical Formulation

The consumption function introduced by Keynes is based on his statement of a "fundamental psychological law" that consumers, on the average, tend to increase their consumption as their income increases, but not as much as the increase in their income.† This statement can be summarized by

$$C = f(Y), \qquad (6\text{-}44)$$

where C is consumption and Y is income. Although Keynes listed a number of factors affecting consumption, he indicated that the income variable, especially disposable income, is the most important one.

A simplified consumption function can be represented as

$$C = a + bY, \qquad (6\text{-}45)$$

where $a > 0$ and $b < 1$. The coefficient b is the marginal propensity to consume. Keynes further assumed that the short-run marginal propensity to consume is less than the long-run marginal propensity to consume, since over the longer period of time a consumer's living standard is more flexible.

One of Keynes's controversial conclusions is that in the long-run a greater proportion of income will be saved as real income increases. A number of aggregate-consumption functions found that the ratio of consumption to disposable income C/Y stays constant over several decades. But on the other hand, cross-section data for the household-consumption pattern shows that the C/Y ratio decreases as income increases. These conflicting findings resulted in a number of modified consumption theories.

Duesenberry's theory, known as the relative-income hypothesis, assumes that an individual's consumption does not depend on his absolute income but rather on his percentile position in the income distribution.‡ Further-

†Keynes, *The General Theory of Employment, Interest, and Money* (New York, Harcourt Brace, 1936).
‡Duesenberry, *Income, Saving, and the Theory of Consumer Behavior* (Cambridge, Harvard University Press, 1952).

more, an individual has the habit of persistence in his consumption pattern, so that he will continue to base his consumption pattern partially on higher previous levels of income if his current income falls. Therefore, Duesenberry's hypothesis can be formulated as

$$\frac{C_t}{Y_t} = a + b\left(\frac{Y_t}{Y^0}\right), \tag{6-46}$$

where C_t and Y_t are current consumption and income and where Y^0 is the peak previous income.

Friedman introduced his permanent-income hypothesis, which assumes that it is an individual's permanent income that affects his consumption.[†] This hypothesis can be formulated as the following:

$$C_p = K(i, w, u)\, Y_p \tag{6-47}$$

$$Y = Y_p + Y_t \qquad \rho(Y_p Y_t) = 0 \qquad \overline{Y}_t = 0 \tag{6-48}$$

$$C = C_p + C_t \qquad \rho(C_p C_t) = 0 \qquad \overline{C}_t = 0 \tag{6-49}$$

$$\rho(Y_t C_t) = 0, \tag{6-50}$$

where Y is the measured income, Y_p is the permanent income, Y_t is the transitory income, C is the measured consumption, C_p is the permanent consumption, C_t is the transitory consumption, K is the marginal propensity to consume between permanent consumption and permanent income (it is also the average propensity to consume), i is the interest rate, w is the ratio of nonhuman wealth to permanent income, u is the other economic and demographic factors affecting K, ρ is the correlation coefficient, and $\overline{Y}_t$ and $\overline{C}_t$ are the mean values of Y_t and C_t.

There are other theories to explain an individual's consumption behavior. Among them the role of wealth in the consumption function, proposed by Ando and Modigliani, is known as life-cycle hypothesis.[‡] This hypothesis assumes that an individual's consumption depends on the resources available to the individual, the rate of return to capital, and the age of the consumer. The effect of

[†] Friedman, *A Theory of the Consumption Function* (Princeton, Princeton University Press, 1957).

[‡] Ando and Modigliani, "The 'Life Cycle' Hypothesis of Saving: Aggregate Implications and Test," *American Economic Review*, Vol. 53 (March 1963), pp. 55–84.

liquid assets on consumption was proposed by Zellner† and others.

6.6.2 Empirical Examples

There are numerous empirical studies on the consumption function. We choose Brown‡ and Zellner§ as two examples.

Brown's work modified Duesenberry's habit-persistence hypothesis by introducing a lagged consumption variable C_{-1} in the model instead of the variable of the previous highest income level. Brown adopted Klein's suggestion on the possible different effects on marginal propensity to consume as a result of wage income (Y_w) or nonwage income (Y_π). Therefore, Brown separated income into these two categories. A dummy variable A^c was introduced in the model to take into account the different possible consumption patterns before and after World War II. A 0 value is designated for the prewar period, and 1 is designated for postwar period. The Canadian aggregate annual data are collected for 1926 to 1941 and 1946 to 1949. Brown's single-equation estimated model is

$$C = 0.9138 + 0.5929Y_w + 0.3419Y_\pi + 0.2000C_{-1}$$
$$(5.5) \quad (8.1) \qquad (5.8) \qquad (2.8)$$
$$+ 0.6958A^c \qquad R^2 = 0.998, \qquad (6\text{-}51)$$
$$(5.1)$$

where the values in parentheses are the t ratios. All variables are measured in billions of constant dollars relative to the period 1935 to 1939.

The results of Equation (6-51) indicate that the marginal propensity to consume with respect to wage income is higher than the marginal propensity to consume from the nonwage income.

At the time, Brown was not aware of the statistical problem caused by the lagged dependent variable in the model. But one can understand that there is a possible bias in the estimates, in view of discussions in Section 5.5.

†Zellner, "The Short-Run Consumption Function," *Econometrica*, Vol. 25 (October 1957), pp. 552–567.

‡Brown, "Habit Persistence and Lags in Consumer Behavior," *Econometrica*, Vol. 20 (July 1952), pp. 355–371.

§ Zellner, *op. cit.*

6.6   Consumption Function

Brown's article also investigated the consumption function based on the simultaneous-equation model. Since in the whole economy, consumption and income are determined simultaneously, the single-equation approach will result in biased estimates. A detailed discussion of this problem is presented in Chapter 7.

Zellner tried to test whether consumers' liquid asset holdings have any effects on consumption.† He formulated a number of alternative consumption functions, and then he set up a number of criteria for selecting the preferable one. The criteria include the expected sign, the standard error of the coefficient, the Durbin–Watson statistic, the adjusted R^2, and the predictive power of the model. Estimates are based on quarterly data in the United States between 1947 and 1955, excluding the third quarter of 1950 and the first quarter of 1951. The ordinary least squares are used. Among these estimated equations the following is a preferred one according to the above criteria:

$$C = -18.96 + 0.375Y + 0.489C_{-1} + 0.219L_{-1}$$
$$\qquad\qquad (0.110) \quad (0.160) \qquad (0.067)$$

$$R^2 = 0.984 \qquad DW = 1.77, \tag{6-52}$$

where the values in parentheses are the standard errors of the coefficient. Equation (6-52) suggested that consumption in the short run is affected by consumers' incomes (Y), lagged consumption (C_{-1}), and lagged liquid assets (L_{-1}). All variables are in billions of dollars.

†*Ibid.*

7

SIMULTANEOUS-EQUATION MODEL

7.1 Introduction

7.1.1 Basic Concepts

We have so far discussed the single-equation estimation. Obviously there are a number of instances in which the use of a single-equation model cannot be justified by economic theory. A standard example is a demand function:

$$Q = a_1 + a_2 P + a_3 Y + U_1 . \qquad (7\text{-}1)$$

Equation (7-1) indicates that the consumer's demand for a given commodity (Q) is a function of its price (P), the consumer's income (Y), and the random disturbance (U_1). However, in the market economy the price of this commodity is determined not only by the supplier but also by the consumer. Indeed, the amount demanded and the amount supplied will determine the equilibrium price, and the price in turn will affect the demand and supply. The empirical data we collected are generated from the completed transactions. In fact, the completed transaction implies that the data are derived from that point at which the amount demanded is equal to the amount supplied (Q_s); hence, the equilibrium point. Equation (7-2) is the equilibrium condition:

$$Q_s = Q. \qquad (7\text{-}2)$$

Therefore, it is clear now that the quantity demanded and the price of the commodity are determined simultaneously in the market. It is in this sense that we should introduce a supply equation in the model:

$$Q_s = b_1 + b_2 P + b_3 W + U_2 . \qquad (7\text{-}3)$$

Equation (7-3) indicates that the supply of a given commodity (Q_s) is a function of its price (P), the weather (W), and the random disturbance (U_2), assuming, for instance, that this is an agricultural commodity. Equations (7-1), (7-2), and (7-3) taken together are called a simultaneous-equation model. This model implies that quantities Q and Q_s and price P are simultaneously determined. This formulation is a more meaningful and logical approach than studying the demand function alone.

The equality condition in Equation (7-2) can help us to simplify the model by substituting Equation (7-2) into Equation (7-3), which then becomes

$$Q = b_1 + b_2 P + b_3 W + U_2 , \qquad (7\text{-}4)$$

thus eliminating Q_s and obtaining two equations, Equations (7-1) and (7-4), with two variables Q and P to be determined.

Before we illustrate a macroeconomic model, it would be worthwhile to discuss some of the basic terminology about the variables in a simultaneous-equation model. The variables of a simultaneous-equation system are classified into two groups. The first group includes those variables whose values or levels must be explained or predicted. Variables in this group are called endogenous variables. The word "endogenous" is derived from the Greek word that means "generated from inside." The second group of variables need not be explained or predicted, because they can be assumed to be determined in advance or fixed when we know the endogenous variables. Variables in this group are called exogenous variables. The word "exogenous" is derived from the Greek word that means "generated from outside." The criterion of this classification is based on the economic theory or assumptions made.

In the market equilibrium model above we consider quantity and price of a given commodity as examples of endogenous variables, since we would like to explain the market determination of these two variables. On the other hand, the income and the weather variables in the model are not determined by the commodity market. These two variables are determined outside of the system. Therefore, these two variables are exogenous variables.

Economics is generally characterized by such simultaneous relationships. Both the market equilibrium and the determination of national income can illustrate this phenomenon. The simple Keynesian model assumes that consumption (C) is a function of income (Y):

$$C = a + bY + V .\qquad(7\text{-}5)$$

However, in the economy as a whole, national income depends on the consumers' demand since their demand determines the level of production. In fact, national income is comprised of two components, consumption and investment I, according to the simple Keynesian model. Thus, there is an identity:

$$Y = C + I .\qquad(7\text{-}6)$$

Equations (7-5) and (7-6), simultaneously, determine both the level of consumption and income. These two equations are called the simple Keynesian income determination model. Within this model, consumption and income are endogenous variables. Investment in this model is assumed to be autonomous, which is independent of income and consumption. Thus, investment is an exogenous variable.

In some cases lagged endogenous variables are introduced into the system. For instance, in the previous discussion of the consumption function the habit-persistence hypothesis assumes that

$$C_t = a + bY_t + cC_{t-1} + V_t ,\qquad(7\text{-}7)$$

where t denotes the time period and V_t is a random disturbance. The model is completed by the identity

$$Y_t = C_t + I_t .\qquad(7\text{-}8)$$

The lagged consumption variable in this model is considered a predetermined variable because this variable is determined in advance, although it is endogenous during the previous period. To simplify the classification of variables we can divide them into endogenous variables and predetermined variables instead of endogenous variables and exogenous variables. In the former classification predetermined variables include exogenous variables and lagged endogenous variables. Therefore, the definition of predetermined variable is broader than that of exogenous variable.

7.1.2 Structural Model and Reduced Form

Since we do not use matrix algebra in this text, the discussions of the structural model and the reduced form rely on the two models illustrated in the previous section:

the market equilibrium model, Equations (7-1) and (7-4), and the simple Keynesian model, Equations (7-5) and (7-6).

The formulation of the market-equilibrium model and the simple Keynesian model are based on the economic theory of the behavior of individuals or firms in the economic structure. The interrelations of these economic units is reflected in the set of equations. Each set of equations is defined as the structural model, and each equation is called a structural equation. The coefficients in the structural equations are called structural coefficients, or structural parameters. The structural model makes sense as an economic theory; therefore, we can use a structural model to test the economic hypotheses. Because the structural model is formulated according to economic theory, it is possible to have endogenous variables appear also on the righthand side of the equation, such as the variables P and Y, respectively, in the two models above. This situation will pose some difficulties in the statistical estimation of the model. The statistical problem can best be examined by the simple Keynesian model, Equations (7-5) and (7-6).

Let us specify Equations (7-5) and (7-6) with time subscripts:

$$C_t = a + bY_t + V_t \qquad (7\text{-}9)$$

and

$$Y_t = C_t + I_t , \qquad (7\text{-}10)$$

where

$$E(V_t) = 0 \qquad (7\text{-}11)$$

and

$$E(V_t V_{t-s}) = \begin{cases} \sigma^2 & \text{for } s = 0 \text{ and for all } t \\ 0 & \text{for } s \neq 0 \text{ and for all } t. \end{cases} \qquad (7\text{-}12)$$

Furthermore, I_t is exogenous and it is distributed independently of V_t. With these assumptions we will find that one of the classical least-squares assumptions is violated between the relations of Y_t and V_t. Y_t and V_t in the consumption equation, Equation (7-9), are correlated. This can be seen as follows.

Substitute Equation (7-9) into Equation (7-10) and solve for Y_t. Then

$$Y_t = \frac{a}{1-b} + \frac{1}{1-b} I_t + \frac{1}{1-b} V_t . \qquad (7\text{-}13)$$

123

Simultaneous-Equation Model

Now the covariance of Y_t and V_t is

$$EY_t V_t = \frac{a}{1-b} E(V_t) + \frac{1}{1-b} E(I_t V_t) + \frac{1}{1-b} E(V_t^2)$$

$$= \frac{1}{1-b} \sigma^2 \quad \text{since } I_t \text{ is independent of } V_t, \\ \text{and by Equations (7-11) and (7-12)}$$

$$\neq 0. \tag{7-14}$$

When Y_t and V_t are correlated, the direct application of the classical least-squares method to Equation (7-9) results in a biased estimate of a and b, as we have shown in Sections 5.4 and 5.5.

Indeed, the classical least-squares estimates in Equation (7-9) will not only be biased but also inconsistent; that is, a bias persists even for infinitely large samples. The algebraic explanation for this follows:

Take the mean value of Equation (7-9). It becomes

$$\overline{C} = a + b\overline{Y} + \overline{V}. \tag{7-15}$$

Equation (7-9) minus Equation (7-15) results in

$$C_t - \overline{C} = b(Y_t - \overline{Y}) + (V_t - \overline{V}). \tag{7-16}$$

Multiplying $(Y_t - Y)$ through Equation (7-16), taking the summation and dividing through by $\Sigma(Y_t - \overline{Y})^2$, Equation (7-16) becomes

$$\hat{b} = b + \frac{\Sigma(V_t - \overline{V})(Y_t - \overline{Y})}{\Sigma(Y_t - \overline{Y})^2} \tag{7-17}$$

where $\hat{b}$ is the classical least-squares estimator and b is the true parameter. Equation (7-17) can be simplified. Then the second term of the expression can be divided by n in both numerator and denominator:

$$\hat{b} = b + \frac{\Sigma V_t(Y_t - \overline{Y})/n}{\Sigma(Y_t - \overline{Y})^2/n} \tag{7-18}$$

where n is the sample size. As the sample size n approaches infinity, the probability limit of the sample covariance between V_t and Y_t tends to be a constant; that is,

$$p \lim_{n \to \infty} \frac{\Sigma V_t(Y_t - \overline{Y})}{n} = EV_t Y_t = \frac{1}{1-b} \sigma^2. \tag{7-19}$$

Similarly the probability limit of the sample variance of Y_t tends to be a constant; that is,

$$p \lim_{n \to \infty} \frac{\Sigma (Y_t - \overline{Y})^2}{n} = E(Y - E(Y))^2 = \sigma_y^2 . \qquad (7\text{-}20)$$

If we substitute Equations (7-19) and (7-20) into (7-18), the probability limit of the least-squares estimator b becomes

$$p \lim_{n \to \infty} \hat{b} = b + \frac{\sigma^2}{(1 - b)\sigma_y^2} . \qquad (7\text{-}21)$$

Since by assumption marginal propensity to consume b lies between 0 and 1 and since variances are always greater than or equal to 0, the second term on the righthand side of Equation (7-21) is positive. Thus,

$$p \lim_{n \to \infty} \hat{b} > b . \qquad (7\text{-}22)$$

Equation (7-22) implies that the classical least-squares estimation will have an asymptotic bias; that is, the bias cannot be eliminated by increasing the sample size. This bias is an upward bias with respect to the true parameter. We also call this bias the simultaneity bias or simultaneous-equation bias.

An economic interpretation of this bias may help us to understand its nature. Equation (7-5) implies that consumption increases because of a change in the factors affecting the disturbance term, as well as because of the effect of income increase. Such an occurrence might be caused by additional expenditures, such as the Vietnam War. Then consumption could rise considerably even if income remained unchanged. However, income would be almost certain to increase, because consumption is one of the determinants of income, provided the additional consumption does not affect investment. The reasoning so far indicates that consumption increases is a result of income and has ignored the portion of the increase in income resulting from random factors that increase consumption and the increase in consumption caused by the increase of income. Therefore, the importance of the income variable in Equation (7-5) is overstated, or in other words, the parameter of the income variable is biased upward. The problem would not arise if income and consumption were independent.

As we can see now that this statistical problem of applying the classical least-squares to the structural equations is caused by the fact that the endogenous variable on the righthand side of the equation is correlated with the disturbance term. One of the methods for treating this problem is to solve Equations (7-5) and (7-6) by expressing each endogenous variable C_t and Y_t as a function of predetermined (or exogenous) variable I_t in the system:

$$C_t = \frac{a}{1-b} + \frac{b}{1-b} I_t + \frac{1}{1-b} V_t \qquad (7\text{-}23)$$

$$Y_t = \frac{a}{1-b} + \frac{1}{1-b} I_t + \frac{1}{1-b} V_t . \qquad (7\text{-}24)$$

In Equations (7-23) and (7-24) I_t is distributed independently of V_t, according to our assumption. We can then apply least squares to estimate Equations (7-23) and (7-24) to obtain consistent estimates for a and b. The method of transformation and the proof of consistency is shown in Section 7.3.

Equations (7-23) and (7-24) are called *reduced-form equations*, equations in which the endogenous variable is expressed in terms of predetermined variables and the disturbance in the system. The set of reduced-form equations is called the reduced form of the model. The coefficients in the reduced-form equations are called the reduced-form coefficients. It can be readily seen that the reduced-form coefficients are functions of the structural coefficients.

The reduced-form equations not only have the advantage of estimating consistent structural coefficients, but they also can be used for forecasting economic phenomena. Again, we use the simple Keynesian model as an example. In the structural equation (7-5) coefficient b is the marginal propensity to consume, which expresses the "direct" relationships between income and consumption. However, the coefficients of I_t in the reduced-form equation (7-24) are the "total" effects of a change in predetermined variable I_t on the endogenous variable Y_t after taking into account of the interdependences among the endogenous variables. The coefficient in Equation (7-24) can also be interpreted as the partial derivative of the endogenous variable Y_t with respect to the predetermined variable I_t, with all other predetermined variables held constant. This can be demonstrated by simple algebra based on Equation (7-24):

$$\frac{\Delta Y}{\Delta I} = \frac{1}{1-b} . \qquad (7\text{-}25)$$

The reader is very familiar with Equation (7-25), for it is called an investment multiplier. Any basic economics textbook discusses this concept.† Therefore, we can say that a reduced-form coefficient is a multiplier, or an impact multiplier as suggested by Goldberger.‡ However, if we learn only the reduced form of a model, we cannot embody known changes in the structure model; we cannot test hypotheses concerning the structural coefficients.

So far we have derived reduced-form equations for the simple Keynesian model. We will use the market-equilibrium model as another example for showing how a reduced-form equation can be derived from the structural equations. If we substitute Equation (7-4) into (7-1), solving for P, we get

$$P = \left(\frac{b_1 - a_1}{a_2 - b_2}\right) - \left(\frac{a_3}{a_2 - b_2}\right) Y + \left(\frac{b_3}{a_2 - b_2}\right) W + \left(\frac{V_2 - V_1}{a_2 - b_2}\right).$$

(7-26)

On the other hand, if we substitute Equation (7-4) into (7-1), solving for Q, we get

$$Q = \left(\frac{-a_1 b_2 + b_1 a_2}{a_2 - b_2}\right) - \left(\frac{b_2 a_3}{a_2 - b_2}\right) Y$$

$$+ \left(\frac{a_2 b_3}{a_2 - b_2}\right) W + \left(\frac{a_2 V_2 - b_2 V_1}{a_2 - b_2}\right). \quad (7\text{-}27)$$

Equations (7-26) and (7-27) are reduced-form equations of Equations (7-1) and (7-4). The reduced-form coefficients in Equations (7-26) and (7-27) are functions of the structural coefficients. As we indicated, in order to obtain consistent estimators for structural coefficients, classical least-squares can be used to estimate the reduced-form coefficients. However, the relationships between reduced-form coefficients and structural coefficients are sometimes very complicated. Therefore, the translation of reduced-form coefficients into structural coefficients is not always straightforward. Sometimes it is impossible. To investigate this transformation problem, we discuss the concept of identification.

†See, for example, Samuelson, *Economics: An Introductory Analysis* (New York, McGraw-Hill, 1969).
‡Goldberger, *Impact Multipliers and Dynamic Properties of the Klein–Goldberger Model* (Amsterdam, North-Holland, 1959).

7.2   Identification

7.2.1   Problem of Identification

We have so far discussed the basic concepts of the simultaneous-equation model.   We have also shown that classical least-squares estimation will result in inconsistent estimators for the structural parameters.   One way to overcome this problem is to derive the reduced-form equation and then, based on the reduced-form coefficient, transform the reduced-form coefficients into structural parameters. *Identification* is the problem of finding a unique solution for the structural parameters from the reduced-form coefficients.   Therefore, identification of the model is logically prior to estimation of the model. If we cannot identify the structural parameters, then the estimation effort will be in vain.

The problem of identification can be divided into two parts.   First there is the logical problem of determining whether the estimated equation is actually the equation specified.   For example, is the function a demand function rather than a supply function?   This is the equation we posed in Section 6.2.   Second, even if we can identify the structural equation, there may be no unique solution for the structural parameters.   Even if one of the structural equations is identified, there is the possibility that some other structural equations are not identified.

Suppose that we want to estimate a demand function. The function specifies that the quantity demanded is a function of its price.   However, as stated above, the collected data of quantity and price variables are the records of equilibrium between demand and supply.   Thus, if we specify that the supply of the commodity is a function of its price, based on the sample data, we will not be able to identify or to distinguish between the demand function and the supply function.   Two-dimensional price-quantity relationships display the phenomenon in Figure 7-1(*a*).

More than a half-century ago Moore estimated the demand for cast iron with a positive slope with respect to its price.† It was Working who pointed out that the simple fit

†Moore, *Economic Cycles: Their Law and Cause* (New York, Macmillan, 1914).

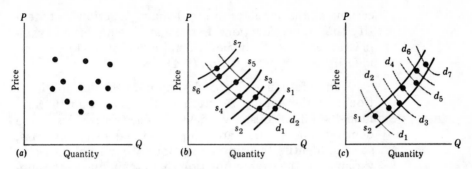

Figure 7-1   Identification of demand and supply curves (a) equilibriums of demand and supply; (b) identification of a demand curve; and (c) identification of a supply curve.

between price and quantity data does not necessarily reveal the demand curve.† In fact, he pointed out that Moore's estimation may be a supply curve. Working reminded us of the importance of identification in empirical estimations.

In order to identify the demand function, we have to assume that the demand for a commodity is stable over time, but the supply of a commodity is fluctuating, such as with agricultural products. It is the shift of the supply function that helps us to trace or to identify the points of the demand curve for the commodity. This is illustrated in Figure 7-1(b). The factors affecting the shift of the supply curve are such things as weather and input costs. These variables are certainly not causing the demand-curve shift. Therefore, it is the specification of the variables in the supply function that identifies the demand function. In our market-equilibrium example the variable W in the supply equation (7-4) helps to identify the demand function, Equation (7-1).

On the other hand, in order to identify the supply function we have to assume that the supply of a commodity is stable over time but that the demand function is fluctuating. It is the shift of the demand function that helps us to trace or to identify the supply curve of the commodity. This is illustrated in Figure 7-1(c). The factors affecting the shift of the demand curve are such things as income or tastes and preferences. These variables are certainly not causing the supply-curve shift. Therefore, it is the specifi-

†Working, "What Do Statistical Demand Curves Show?" *Quarterly Journal of Economics*, Vol. 41 (February 1927), pp. 212–235.

cations of the variables in the demand function that identify the supply function. In the market-equilibrium example the variable Y in the demand equation (7-1) helps to identify the supply equation (7-4).

Therefore, in order to identify both the demand function and the supply function in the market-equilibrium model simultaneously, we have to specify variables in the demand function that are unique to the demand relations, so as to identify the supply function. We must also specify variables in the supply function that are unique to the supply relations so as to identify the demand function. In fact, the restriction of certain variables to the demand or supply functions plays a fundamental role in identifying the simultaneous-equation model. This point is further elaborated in the remainder of the section.

The foregoing discussions provide an economic explanation of the problem of identification. Now the basic algebraic problem of identification must be discussed. This is the problem of identifying the structural parameters from the reduced-form coefficients. In some instances the transformation from the reduced-form coefficients to structural parameters has a unique solution. This is called a just-identified model. In some cases the transformation from reduced-form coefficients to structural parameters has more than one solution. This is called an overidentified model. Finally, in some instances there is no solution for transforming the reduced-form coefficients to the structural parameters. This is called an underidentified model.

We will use the market-equilibrium model and the simple Keynesian model to show the algebraic problem of identification. The reduced form of the market-equilibrium model is shown by Equations (7-26) and (7-27). When we use the classical least squares to estimate Equations (7-26) and (7-27), we obtain

$$P = \hat{\alpha}_1 + \hat{\alpha}_2 Y + \hat{\alpha}_3 W \qquad (7\text{-}28)$$

and

$$Q = \hat{\beta}_1 + \hat{\beta}_2 Y + \hat{\beta}_3 W , \qquad (7\text{-}29)$$

where

130

$$\hat{\alpha}_1 = \frac{b_1 - a_1}{a_2 - b_2} \qquad \hat{\alpha}_2 = \frac{-a_3}{a_2 - b_2} \qquad \hat{\alpha}_3 = \frac{b_3}{a_2 - b_2}$$

and
$$\hat{\beta}_1 = \frac{-a_1 b_2 + b_1 a_2}{a_2 - b_2} \qquad \hat{\beta}_2 = \frac{-b_2 a_3}{a_2 - b_2} \qquad \hat{\beta}_3 = \frac{a_2 b_3}{a_2 - b_2}.$$

The identification problem of this model is to obtain the solutions for structural parameters of $a_1, a_2, a_3, b_1, b_2,$ and b_3 from the reduced-form coefficients $\hat{\alpha}_1, \hat{\alpha}_2, \hat{\alpha}_3, \hat{\beta}_1, \hat{\beta}_2,$ and $\hat{\beta}_3$. The necessary condition for the solutions are six unknowns and six equations. We notice that

$$\frac{\hat{\beta}_2}{\hat{\alpha}_2} = \hat{b}_2 \quad \text{and} \quad \frac{\hat{\beta}_3}{\hat{\alpha}_3} = \hat{a}_2. \tag{7-30}$$

Therefore, we also obtain the value $(a_2 - b_2)$ for the denominator of each reduced-form coefficient. Thus

$$\hat{a}_3 = (\hat{a}_2 - \hat{b}_2) \frac{\hat{\beta}_2}{\hat{b}_2} \tag{7-31}$$

and

$$\hat{b}_3 = (\hat{a}_2 - \hat{b}_2) \frac{\hat{\beta}_3}{\hat{a}_2}. \tag{7-32}$$

Now we have remaining only a_1 and b_1 to be determined. Based on $\hat{\alpha}_1$ we can write

$$a_1 = \hat{\alpha}_1 (\hat{a}_2 - \hat{b}_2) - b_1. \tag{7-33}$$

Based on $\hat{\beta}_1$ we can write

$$-a_1 \hat{b}_2 + b_1 \hat{a}_2 = \hat{\beta}_1 (\hat{a}_2 - \hat{b}_2). \tag{7-34}$$

If we substitute Equation (7-33) into Equation (7-34), we obtain

$$\hat{b}_1 = \hat{\beta}_1 - \hat{b}_2 \hat{\alpha}_1, \tag{7-35}$$

and finally,

$$\hat{a}_1 = \hat{b}_1 - \hat{\alpha}_1 (\hat{a}_2 - \hat{b}_2). \tag{7-36}$$

Therefore, we have a solution for $a_1, a_2, a_3, b_1, b_2,$ and b_3 based on $\alpha_1, \alpha_2, \alpha_3, \beta_1, \beta_2,$ and β_3. This is the case of the just-identified model.

The reduced-form equations for the simple Keynesian model are shown in Equations (7-23) and (7-24). When we estimate by classical least squares we get

$$C_t = \delta_1 + \delta_2 I_t, \tag{7-37}$$

where

$$\delta_1 = a/(1 - b)$$

and

$$\delta_2 = b/(1 - b).$$

The solution for b is

$$\hat{b} = \frac{\hat{\delta}_2}{1 + \hat{\delta}_2}. \qquad (7\text{-}38)$$

Based on the solution of b, we can obtain

$$\hat{a} = \hat{\delta}_1(1 - \hat{b}). \qquad (7\text{-}39)$$

Therefore, we also have a solution for the structural parameters. The model is also just-identified.

The case of an underidentified model can be illustrated by the market-equilibrium example. Suppose that the supply equation (7-4) omits the W variable, so that it becomes

$$Q = b_1 + b_2 P + U_2. \qquad (7\text{-}40)$$

Therefore, the W variable would not appear in the reduced-form equations (7-28) and (7-29). Although one still can obtain $\hat{b}_2$ by dividing the coefficients of the Y variable, it would be impossible to obtain a_1, a_2, a_3, and b_1. Thus, in the market-equilibrium model Equations (7-1) and (7-40) are underidentified. In fact, if any one equation in the model is underidentified (or not identified), the model is said to be underidentified.

On the other hand, if we add a taste variable as approximated by time trend T in the demand equation (7-1),

$$Q = a_1 + a_2 P + a_3 Y + a_4 T + U_1, \qquad (7\text{-}41)$$

but leave the supply equation (7-4) as it is, then the T variable will be added to each of the reduced-form equations (7-28) and (7-29), $\hat{\alpha}_4 T$ and $\hat{\beta}_4 T$, where

$$\alpha_4 = \frac{b_2 a_4}{a_2 - b_2} \quad \text{and} \quad \hat{\beta}_4 = \frac{a_4}{a_2 - b_2}.$$

We now can obtain

$$\hat{b}_2 = (\hat{\beta}_4 / \hat{\alpha}_4).$$

But Equation (7-30) shows that we can also obtain $\hat{b}_2$ by $\hat{\beta}_2 / \hat{\alpha}_2$, since the structural coefficients $\hat{a}_1, \hat{a}_3, \hat{a}_4, \hat{b}_1$, and $\hat{b}_3$ are all dependent on the value of $\hat{b}_2$. The two estimates of $\hat{b}_2$ will result in different values for other structural parameters. Therefore, the solutions for the structural parameters are not unique but multiple. This is overidentification. In general, a model is said to be overidentified if any one equation in it is overidentified.

It is obvious now that identification is a necessary step before we proceed to estimate the model. If the model is underidentified, then there is no solution for the structural parameters. Thus, we cannot estimate the model properly. If the model is just-identified, then there is a unique solution for the structural parameters. If the model is overidentified, then there are multiple solutions for the structural parameters. However, it is still possible to estimate the model. In general, we call a model identified if it is either just-identified or overidentified. The detailed estimation method is discussed in Section 7.3.

7.2.2 Methods of Identification

We have discussed the concept of identification and some examples of identification. But we find that the algebraic method of identification from reduced-form coefficients to structure parameters is often quite tedious. We have used only two equation models. However, in the case of five or ten equation models it becomes very difficult, if not impossible, to use the algebraic transformation procedure. Therefore, it is useful to discuss the general principles of identification from which we can derive some theorems of identification.

The examples in the previous section suggest that there are two basic principles to identify a simultaneous equation model. First, a logically complete model should have an equal number of endogenous variables and structural equations. This is a necessary requirement for a complete model. The structural model can contain the behavioral equations, such as Equations (7-1) and (7-2), and the definition identity equation, such as Equation (7-3). In this basic market equilibrium model there are three endogenous variables, Q, Q_s, P, and three equations. Second, a set of equations can be identified only if we possess the necessary *a priori* restrictions for each equation; that is, if each equation is known in advance to be sufficiently distinctive from the others. This can be reiterated by the market-equilibrium example in Equations (7-1) and (7-4). We can rewrite a general form as

$$Q = a_1 + a_2 P + a_3 Y + a_4 W + U_1$$

133

and

$$Q_s = b_1 + b_2 P + b_3 W + b_4 Y + U_2.$$

The *a priori* restriction for the demand equation is that $a_4 = 0$. The *a priori* restriction for the supply equation is that $b_4 = 0$. This restriction implies that a certain variable does not play an economic role in a given equation. This kind of *a priori* restriction helps to set the necessary conditions for the identification of any one equation in the model.

Next, for an equation to be identified the number of predetermined (or exogenous) variables K excluded from the equation must be at least greater than or equal to $m - 1$, where m is the number of endogenous variables in the equation.

This is called the order condition of identifiability, or the counting rule. But this is only a necessary, not a sufficient, condition. Based on our market-equilibrium example, Equations (7-1) and (7-4), we find that in Equation (7-1) the predetermined variable excluded in the equation is W, so $K = 1$. There are two endogenous variables in Equation (7-1), Q and P, so $m - 1 = 2 - 1 = 1$. When $K = m - 1$, the model is called just-identified. Thus, Equation (7-1) is just-identified. In Equation (7-4) the predetermined variable Y is excluded; thus $K = 1$; while Equation (7-4) also has two endogenous variables, so $m - 1 = 1$. Therefore, Equation (7-4) is also just-identified. When each equation in the model is just-identified, the model is just-identified.

On the other hand, if we choose Equations (7-1) and (7-40) as the market-equilibrium model, we will find that there is no predetermined variable excluded from Equation (7-1), so $K = 0$, while Equation (7-1) still has two endogenous variables, Q and P, so $m - 1 = 1$. When $K < m - 1$, we say this equation is underidentified, or not identified. Although Equation (7-40) is just-identified, since $K = 1$ and $m = 1$, the model is not identified. The economic interpretation here can be related to the discussion of the previous section wherein the shift variable in the demand function, Equation (7-1), helps to identify the supply function. However, there is no shift variable in the supply function, Equation (7-40). Thus the demand function is not identified.

If we choose Equations (7-41) and (7-4) as the market-equilibrium model, we will find that there is one predetermined variable excluded from Equation (7-41), so $K = 1$, while $m - 1 = 1$ for Equation (7-41).   Thus, $K = m - 1$.   But in comparing Equation (7-4), we will find that there are two predetermined variables excluded from the equation, so $K = 2$.   However, Equation (7-4) still has two endogenous variables, so $m - 1 = 1$.   In this case $K > m - 1$.   When an equation has $K > m - 1$ it is called overidentified.   Equation (7-4) is overidentified, so the model is overidentified.   This finding corresponds to the algebraic solution of identification between reduced-form coefficients and structural parameters shown in the previous section.

This counting role of identification reveals a much simpler method of identification than the algebraic solution between reduced-form coefficients and structural parameters.   But this rule of identification satisfies only the necessary condition.   The sufficient condition is also called the rank condition of identifiability.   The formal statement of the rank condition is in terms of matrix algebraic concepts.   Interested students may consult Goldberger for a detailed discussion of identification rules in terms of matrix notation.†

The drawback of the rank condition is that one has to form a reduced-form matrix and then examine the rank of a relevant submatrix.   If a model is relatively large, the examination of the rank condition is very tedious.   Thus, in most of the cases the counting rule is more widely used than the rank condition.

7.3   Estimation Methods

7.3.1   Indirect Least-Squares

This estimation method is used when the model is just-identified; that is, when there is a unique solution for transforming the structural parameters from the reduced-form coefficients.   As we indicated in Section 7.1, the classical least-squares estimation for the structural equations are biased.   One way to obtain a consistent estimate for the

†Goldberger, *Econometric Theory* (New York, Wiley, 1964), pp. 306–314.

Simultaneous-Equation Model

structural parameters is to apply the classical least-squares to the reduced-form equation. If the transformation from reduced-form coefficients to structural parameters has a unique solution, then the estimated structural coefficients will be consistent.

We use the simple Keynesian model as an example to show the argument above. When we take the expected value of the reduced form Equation (7-23), we get

$$E(C_t) = E\left(\frac{a}{1-b}\right) + E\left(\frac{b}{1-b}\right)I_t + E\left(\frac{1}{1-b}V_t\right)$$

$$= \frac{a}{1-b} + \frac{b}{1-b}I_t$$

since $E(V_t) = 0$, by Equation (7-11).

Suppose that we estimate it by classical least-squares. We get

$$C_t = \delta_1 + \delta_2 I_t + \epsilon_t, \qquad (7\text{-}42)$$

where

$$\delta_1 = \frac{a}{1-b}, \qquad \delta_2 = \frac{b}{1-b}, \qquad \epsilon_t = \frac{V_t}{1-b}.$$

The disturbance is assumed to have 0 mean and constant variance, as indicated in Equations (7-11) and (7-12). Furthermore I_t and V_t are uncorrelated. Therefore, classical least squares will result in unbiased estimates of δ_1 and δ_2. However, both a and b are nonlinear functions of δ_1 and δ_2. The relations are

$$\hat{b} = \frac{\hat{\delta}_2}{1 + \hat{\delta}_2}$$

and

$$\hat{a} = \hat{\delta}_1(1 - \hat{b}).$$

Thus, both $\hat{a}$ and $\hat{b}$ are not unbiased when $\hat{a}$ and $\hat{b}$ are obtained from $\hat{\delta}_1$ and $\hat{\delta}_2$. Only when the sample size increases then the probability limit of the above two equations becomes

$$p\lim \hat{b} = \frac{p\lim \hat{\delta}_2}{p\lim (1 + \hat{\delta}_2)}$$

$$= \frac{b/(1-b)}{1 + b/(1-b)}$$

$$= b, \qquad (7\text{-}43)$$

and

$$p \lim \hat{a} = p \lim \hat{\delta}_1 \cdot p \lim (1 - \hat{b})$$

$$= \frac{a}{1 - b} \cdot (1 - b)$$

$$= a. \tag{7-44}$$

When a and b are consistent, then a and b will also be asymptotically unbiased. Let us now summarize the steps of indirect least squares. First, when the model is just-identified, we apply classical least squares to estimate the reduced-form coefficients of the model. Second, based on the estimated reduced-form coefficients, we can obtain the structural parameters. The solutions of structural parameters are unique and statistically consistent.

7.3.2   Two-Stage Least-Squares

The reason for using indirect least squares to estimate the reduced-form equation is to obtain unbiased estimates of reduced-form coefficients, since in the structural model one or more of the explanatory variables may be endogenous and so may correlate with the error term. However, the indirect least squares will be useful provided that the structural parameters have a unique solution from the reduced-form coefficients. In the case of the overidentified model there are multiple solutions for structural parameters from the reduced-form coefficients. Therefore, the indirect least-squares technique will not be helpful in the overidentified case. In order to overcome the correlation problem between the endogenous explanatory variable and the error term in the structural equation, Theil and others suggested the two-stage least-squares technique.† This estimation method has been widely used in empirical work.

The objective of the two-stage least-squares technique is to make the explanatory endogenous variable uncorrelated with the error term, such that the direct application of classical least squares to structural equations will result in consistent estimates. In this case the possible multiple solution for structural parameters derived from the reduced-form coefficients can be avoided. We will have a unique solution for the structural parameters subject to

---

†Theil, *Estimation and Simultaneous Correlation in Complete Equation Systems* (The Hague, Centraal Planbureau, 1953).

the initial choice of the explanatory endogenous variable estimated in the first-stage least squares. The estimation procedures can be illustrated by the simple Keynesian model, for simplicity's purpose.

Let

$$C_t = a + bY_t + V_t$$

and

$$Y_t = C_t + I_t,$$

where Y_t and V_t are correlated but I_t and V_t are uncorrelated. Therefore, in the first stage if we formulate

$$Y_t = d_1 + d_2 I_t + e_t, \tag{7-45}$$

Equation (7-45) will result in

$$\hat{d}_2 = \frac{\sum y_t i_t}{\sum i_t^2} \tag{7-46}$$

where y_t and i_t are deviations from their respective means. Then

$$\hat{d}_1 = \overline{Y}_t - \hat{d}_2 \overline{I}_t.$$

Thus,

$$\hat{Y}_t = \hat{d}_1 + \hat{d}_2 I_t.$$

The estimated $\hat{Y}_t$ will be uncorrelated with V_t or e_t since $\hat{Y}_t$ is a function of I_t. Therefore, the second stage is

$$C_t = a + b(\hat{Y}_t + e_t) + V_t$$
$$= a + b\hat{Y}_t + (be_t + V_t). \tag{7-47}$$

Since $\hat{Y}$ is uncorrelated with e_t and V_t, so least squares can be used to estimate a and b:

$$\hat{b} = \frac{\sum \hat{y}_t c_t}{\sum \hat{y}_t^2} \tag{7-48}$$

and

$$\hat{a} = \overline{C}_t - \hat{b}\,\overline{Y}_t, \tag{7-49}$$

where c_t is deviations from its mean. Indeed, Goldberger shows that if the model is just-identified, the results from two-stage least-squares technique are identical to the indirect least-squares technique.[†]

†Goldberger, *Econometric Theory* (New York, Wiley, 1964), pp. 329–336.

We now use the overidentified market-equilibrium model to recapitulate the procedures of two-stage least-squares technique.   The model is Equation (7-41) and (7-4):

$$Q = a_1 + a_2 P + a_3 Y + a_4 T + U_1$$
$$Q = b_1 + b_2 P + b_3 W + U_2.$$

Since P is correlated with U_1 and U_2 in the model, the first stage is to regress P as a function of all predetermined variables Y, T, and W. The implicit function will be

$$P = f(Y, T, W, e), \qquad (7\text{-}50)$$

where e is the error term. The classical least-squares estimation will yield $\hat{P}$ from Equation (7-50). The estimated $\hat{P}$ is not correlated with U_1 and U_2. Therefore, the second stage is to substitute $\hat{P}$ for P into Equations (7-41) and (7-4). This will allow all the variables on the righthand side of the equation to be uncorrelated with error terms in the equation. The model becomes

$$Q = a_1 + a_2 \hat{P} + a_3 Y + a_4 T + (a_2 e + U_1) \qquad (7\text{-}51)$$
$$Q = b_1 + b_2 \hat{P} + b_3 W + (b_2 e + U_2). \qquad (7\text{-}52)$$

We then apply the classical least-squares technique to Equations (7-51) and (7-52).   The estimated structural parameters will be consistent.

It can be seen that the two-stage least-squares technique is a straightforward technique. It can be applied to a single equation at a time. In fact this technique is similar to the instrumental variable estimation discussed in Section 5.4.2.   Goldberger shows that the results of these two estimation techniques are identical.†

7.3.3 Limited-information Method

The limited-information estimation method is also applied to a single equation at a time without requiring us to undertake any estimation for the remaining structural equations. The limited-information method is significant in that we do not make use of the *a priori* restrictions that pertain to equations other than the one being estimated. The minimal information we need is the specification of all predetermined variables that enter the equations other than the equation we are estimating.

†*Ibid.*

Simultaneous-Equation Model

The estimation procedures can be illustrated by the simple Keynesian model. If we compare the following two equations,

$$C_t = a + bY_t + V_t \tag{7-53}$$

$$C_t = a + bY_t + dI_t + U_t, \tag{7-54}$$

then the proper form of the consumption function is to force $d = 0$. However, in the estimation of Equation (7-54) based on sample data, we will likely obtain a nonzero value for d. Furthermore, the sum of squares of the residuals, ΣU_t^2, is smaller than ΣV_t^2. In other words, the residual variance $\bar{U}_t$ will be smaller than the residual variance of V_t. The limited-information method is designed to find an estimator of b such that the ratio of the variance of V_t and U_t is minimized. Thus, this method is also called the least-variance ratio.

$$V_t = C_t - a - bY_t. \tag{7-55}$$

$$U_t = C_t - a - bY_t - dI_t. \tag{7-56}$$

The deviation form of Equations (7-55) and (7-56) are

$$V_t = c_t - by_t \tag{7-57}$$

and

$$U_t = c_t - by_t - di_t. \tag{7-58}$$

Thus

$$V_t = U_t + di_t. \tag{7-59}$$

The least-squares estimator of d from Equation (7-59) is

$$\hat{d} = \frac{\sum V_t i_t}{\sum i_t^2}, \tag{7-60}$$

where V_t and i_t are deviations from their respective means. The variance ratio between V_t and U_t can be expressed as

$$\frac{\sum V_t^2}{\sum U_t^2} = \frac{\sum V_t^2}{\sum (V_t - di_t)^2}$$

$$= \frac{\sum V_t^2}{\sum V_t^2 - \dfrac{\left(\sum V_t i_t\right)^2}{\sum i_t^2}}. \tag{7-61}$$

In order to let $\Sigma V_t^2 / \Sigma U_t^2$ become minimum, given that $\Sigma U_t^2 < \Sigma V_t^2$, the limit of the ratio will be 1. This implies that if $(\Sigma V_t i_t)^2 / \Sigma i_t^2 = 0$, the minimum condition can be achieved. Σi_t^2 is always positive. Thus, $\Sigma V_t i_t$ should be 0. Therefore,

$$\sum (c_t - by_t) i_t = 0 \tag{7-62}$$

or

$$\sum c_t i_t - b \sum y_t i_t = 0$$

and

$$\hat{b} = \frac{\sum c_t i_t}{\sum y_t i_t}. \tag{7-63}$$

Notice that the estimator of the limited-information method is identical to the instumental-variable estimation shown in Section 5.3.7. Therefore, it is also identical to the two-stage least-squares estimation. However, this situation represents a special case when the model is just-identified. When the model is overidentified, these three methods result in different estimates.

7.3.4 System Method

The system method is to estimate the structural equations simultaneously. In other words, this method is used to estimate the structural parameters, taking into account all *a priori* restrictions for every equation in the system. There are two general methods for the system estimation. One is the maximum-likelihood method and the second is the three-stage least-squares method.

The full-information maximum-likelihood method was developed by Koopmans, Rubin, and Leipnik.† They use the maximum-likelihood principle to obtain the structural parameters under all the restrictions in the structural equations by assuming that the structural disturbances are normally distributed. The development of this method relies on the differential calculus of the matrix notation. Interested students may consult Goldberger.‡

†Koopmans, Rubin, and Leipnik, "Measuring the Equation Systems of Dynamic Economics," chap. 2 in *Statistical Inference in Dynamic Economic Models*, Cowles Commission Monograph 10, T. C. Koopmans, ed. (New York, Wiley, 1950), pp. 53–237.

‡Goldberger, *op. cit.*, pp. 352–356.

The advantage of the full-information maximum-likelihood estimation is that these estimates are consistent and efficient. They are sometimes, but not always, unbiased. However, this method has one major disadvantage. Because of the complex calculations of this method, it has rarely been used, especially since the introduction of two-stage least-squares and three-stage least-squares methods.

The three-stage least-squares method was developed by Zellner and Theil.† This method makes use of information of all predetermined variables in the model and estimates the structural equations simultaneously. The method of incorporating the predetermined-variable information into each structural equation is to multiply the predetermined variables throughout each structural equation. However, this transformation will lead to a possible nonconstant-error variance for each structural equation. In order to correct this situation, when we estimate the model by the two-stage least-squares method, we use the residuals from the two-stage least-squares estimates as a weighting factor and perform the weighted regression as discussed in Section 5.3.

Thus, the three-stage least-squares method is an extension of the two-stage least-squares method. The third stage is the application of a weighted regression, or the so-called generalized least squares, to correct for possible heteroscedasticity in the simultaneous-equation model. Again, the weights are obtained from the residuals of the two-stage least-squares estimates.

7.4 Applications of the Simultaneous-Equation Model

7.4.1 Microeconomic Model

The pioneer work on the microeconomic simultaneous-equation model was done by Girshick and Haavelmo on the demand for food.‡ In fact, most of the microeconomic simultaneous-equation models are in the area of

†Zellner and Theil, "Three-Stage Least Squares: Simultaneous Estimation of Simultaneous Equations," *Econometrica*, Vol. 30 (January 1962), pp. 54–78.

‡Girshick and Haavelmo, "Statistical Analysis of the Demand for Food: Examples of Simultaneous Estimation of Structural Equations," *Econometrics*, Vol. 15 (April 1947), pp. 79–116.

agricultural products. The United States Department of Agriculture engaged in extensive studies on the demand for various farm products by using the simultaneous-equation model; Fox was one of the important contributors to this research. This section uses one of his studies as an example.†

Fox studied the demand for pork in the United States from 1922 to 1941. He formulated the following demand and supply equations for pork:

$$Q = a_1 + b_1 P + c_1 Y + U \qquad (7\text{-}64)$$

and

$$Q = a_2 + b_2 P + c_2 Z + V, \qquad (7\text{-}65)$$

where P is the retail price of pork, Q is the consumption of pork, Y is the disposable consumer income, and Z is an estimate of pork production predetermined before the current period. There are two endogenous variables, Q and P, in the model. Y is considered as exogenous in the system since the expenditures on meat as a whole represent only 2 or 3% of disposable personal income. Thus, it is difficult to see how the consumption of pork products will affect the national income to any significant degree. Z is considered as predetermined, since 90% of the variation in pork production was attributable to predetermined variables, such as weather and disease conditions. Furthermore, the time span between sow breeding and hog slaughter is about 12 to 13 months; thus there is very little latitude to change the current-year production.

Fox transforms all the variables to logarithmic form. Then he takes the first differences of logarithms of annual observations of the period 1922 to 1941. According to the rules of identification, this model is just-identified. Fox derived reduced-form equations in terms of Q and P. The classical least-squares method can be applied to the reduced-form equation. The estimated reduced-form equations are

$$Q = 0.0026 - 0.0018Y + 0.6839Z \qquad R^2 = 0.89 \qquad (7\text{-}66)$$
$$ (0.0673) \quad (0.0582)$$

†Fox, *The Analysis of Demand for Farm Products*, Technical Bulletin No. 1081 (Washington, U.S. Department of Agriculture, 1953).

and

$$P = -0.0101 + 1.0813Y - 0.8320Z \qquad R^2 = 0.893. \quad \text{(7-67)}$$
$$\quad\;\; (0.1339) \quad (0.1159)$$

The values in the parentheses are standard errors of the reduced-form coefficients. The transformation of the reduced-form coefficients to structural parameters are

$$a_1 = -0.0063, \qquad a_2 = 0.0026,$$
$$b_1 = -0.8220, \qquad b_2 = -0.0017,$$

and

$$c_1 = 0.8870, \qquad c_2 = 0.6825.$$

Thus, the structural equations can be written as

$$Q = -0.0063 - 0.8220P + 0.8870Y + U \qquad \text{(7-68)}$$
$$Q = 0.0026 - 0.0017P + 0.6825Z + V. \qquad \text{(7-69)}$$

Because all variables are in logarithmic form, the coefficients are elasticities with respect to each of the explanatory variables. Thus, the elasticity of demand for pork with respect to its price is -0.822, whereas the elasticity of demand for pork with respect to consumers' income is 0.887. However, Fox cautioned that the implication of the results are only particular to that sample period. One should be very careful when trying to extrapolate the estimates to a later time period, since the demand and supply structure changes over the time. Statistical analysis of demand and supply provides only simple and usable information to make forecasts or interpretations within a given range of probability.

Based on the justification that current pork production may not quite respond to its current price, Fox investigated a single-equation model for the demand for pork. Thus, he estimated the structural equations (7-64) and (7-65) by classical least-squares methods, treating P as the dependent variable but Q as an independent variable. His estimates were

$$P = -0.0070 - 1.2518Q + 1.0754Y \qquad R^2 = 0.956. \quad \text{(7-70)}$$
$$\quad\;\; (0.1032) \quad (0.0861)$$

By transformation of Equation (7-68), variable P is expressed as

$$P = -0.0070 - 1.2165Q + 1.0791Y. \qquad \text{(7-71)}$$

Thus, Equations (7-70) and (7-71) are almost identical. On the other hand, when the same technique is applied to the supply equation, the least-squares estimates are

$$Q = 0.002 - 0.0788P + 0.6090Z \qquad R^2 = 0.910, \quad (7\text{-}72)$$
$$(0.0522) \quad (0.0734)$$

where P is not statistically significant and has the wrong sign. Equations (7-69) and (7-72) are quite different. However, when Fox dropped the P variable, the least-squares estimates of Equation (7-72) become

$$Q = 0.0025 + 0.6841Z \qquad R^2 = 0.898, \qquad (7\text{-}73)$$
$$(0.0857)$$

where the coefficient of Z is almost identical to the coefficient of Z in Equation (7-69). Thus, he concluded that the alternative way to study the demand for pork is to assume that supply is predetermined in the current period and that it is the quantity supplied that will influence current price. Current price will not affect current supply. Thus, the alternative formulation of the demand for pork can be expressed by Equation (7-71). Then the classical least-squares method will yield results for Equation (7-71) identical to those for Equation (7-68).

7.4.2   Macroeconomic Model

The simultaneous-equation system was used much earlier in macroeconomic analysis than in microeconomic models. Tinbergen developed a simultaneous equation model to study the business cycle in the United States.[†] Then, in 1950 Klein published a 12-equation model of the United States economy using annual data for the period 1921 to 1941.[‡] A few years later Klein and Goldberger published a 20-equation model, using annual data for 1929 to 1952.[§] In recent times, since 1965 The Brookings Institution has published approximately 350 equations for the United States economy, based on 32 producer sectors. Other large-scale models were also published by the Federal Reserve System and the MIT model (1968), the Wharton School Model (1967), and the United States Department of

[†]Tinbergen, *Statistical Testing of Business Cycle Theories II* (Geneva, League of Nations, 1939).
[‡]Klein, *Economic Fluctuations in the United States 1921–1941*, Cowles Commission Monograph 11 (New York, Wiley, 1950).
[§]Klein and Goldberger, *An Econometric Model of the United States 1929–1952* (Amsterdam, North-Holland, 1955).

Commerce, the OBE Model (1966). These models were used to analyze the workings of the economy and also to forecast future aggregate economic quantities.

This section does not introduce these models in detail. For purposes of illustration we use Christ's small-scale United States economy.† Christ constructed a seven-equation linear econometric model for 1929 to 1941 and 1946 to 1959. He used classical least-squares, two-stage least-squares, and limited-information methods to obtain the structural parameters. The comparison of different kinds of estimation methods are also presented in his example. He developed a theoretical formulation showing how the final model was chosen. His model is centered around the consumption function and the private domestic investment equations. The monetary and financial sectors are ignored. No production function is included. All the variables are measured in 1954 dollars, deflated by the GNP implicit deflator.

The final model is summarized as follows:

Consumption:

$$C = a_0 + a_1 Y + a_2 C_{-1} + U_1. \qquad (7\text{-}74)$$

Investment:

$$I = b_0 + b_1 X_1 + b_2 I_{-1} + b_3 A_{-1} + b_4 A_{-2} + b_5 K_{-1} + U_2. \qquad (7\text{-}75)$$

Labor:

$$W = c_0 + c_1 X_1 + c_2 W_{-1} + U_3. \qquad (7\text{-}76)$$

Corporate saving:

$$S = d_0 + d_1 P + d_2 S_{-1} + d_3 P_{-1} + U_4. \qquad (7\text{-}77)$$

Identities:

$$X_1 + X_2 = C + I + G, \qquad (7\text{-}78)$$

$$X_1 + X_2 = Y + T_1 + S + T_2 + D, \qquad (7\text{-}79)$$

and

$$P + W + X_2 = Y + T_1 + S. \qquad (7\text{-}80)$$

Equations (7-74) through (7-80) represent the complete model. However, Christ introduced an alternative invest-

†Christ, *Econometric Models and Methods* (New York, Wiley, 1968).

7.4 Application of the Simultaneous-Equation Model

ment function as a substitute for Equation (7-75):

$$I = e_0 + e_1 X_1 + e_2 P + e_3 A_{-1} + e_4 A_{-2} + e_5 K_{-1} + U_4,$$
$$(7\text{-}81)$$

where the endogenous variables are

C = real-consumption expenditures,
Y = real-disposable personal income,
I = real-gross private domestic investment,
X_1 = real-gross business product,
W = real-labor income in business including government enterprise and the imputed labor income of proprietors,
S = real-net corporate saving,
P = real-property income net of depreciation and corporate income tax liability.

The predetermined variables are lagged $(-1, -2)$ endogenous variables and the other predetermined variables are as follows:

A_{-1} = stock market price index on December 31 of the preceding year (Standard and Poor) relative to the GNP deflator,
K_{-1} = real net private domestic capital stock on December 31 of the preceding year,
X_2 = real-labor income in general government,
T_1 = real personal tax and nontax payment,
T_2 = real direct business taxes and corporate tax liability plus statistical discrepancy less subsidies,
D = real capital consumption at replacement cost.

The following parameters are presumed to be positive based on economic theory: $a_1, a_2, b_1, b_2, b_3, c_1, c_2, d_1,$ $d_2, e_1, e_2,$ and e_3. The following parameters are presumed to be negative based on economic theory: $b_4, b_5, d_3, e_4,$ and e_5. The model has seven equations and seven endogenous variables. The model satisfies the order condition of identifiability; however, it is overidentified. The classical least-squares method is not strictly applicable to the overidentified simultaneous equation model. However, the statistical estimates from the classical least-squares and two-stage least-squares methods are very close. Thus, Christ used the classical least-squares method as a simple technique to choose among alternative forms of the equation for the final model. The following results are

147

estimated from the classical least-squares, two-stage least-squares, and the limited-information methods. S is the standard error of the estimate, R^2 is the coefficient of determination, and d is the Durbin–Watson statistic. Values in the parentheses are estimated t ratios.

The results show that both the classical least-squares estimates and the two-stage least-squares estimates have smaller values of the standard error of the estimate compared to the limited-information estimation. Since the classical least-squares estimate gives inconsistent estimates and since the limited information method gives the wrong sign in the investment function, Equation (7-81), Christ adopted the two-stage least-squares estimates to derive the reduced-form coefficients. Based on the derived reduced-form coefficients, he made predictions for the United States economy.

Consumption, based on Equation (7-74):

Least squares
$$C = 5.35 + 0.661Y$$
$$(11.6) \quad (4.1)$$
$$+ 0.275C_{-1}$$
$$(2.91)$$
$$S = 2.671 \quad R^2 = 0.998$$

Two-stage
least squares
$$C = 5.68 + 0.686Y$$
$$(1.76)(11.6)$$
$$+ 0.246C_{-1}$$
$$(3.5)$$
$$S = 2.682 \quad d = 1.76$$

Limited-information
least squares
$$C = 6.28 + 0.732Y$$
$$(3.3) \quad (11.8)$$
$$+ 0.193C_{-1}$$
$$(2.64)$$
$$S = 2.756 \quad d = 1.69$$

Investment, based on Equation (7-75):

Least squares
$$I = -21.78 + 0.193X_1$$
$$(-3.7) \quad (7.2)$$
$$+ 0.283I_{-1} + 0.511A_{-1}$$
$$(2.10) \qquad (3.6)$$
$$- 0.338A_{-2} - 0.127K_{-1}$$
$$(-2.00) \qquad (-4.3)$$
$$S = 4.089 \quad R^2 = 0.962$$

7.4 · Application of the Simultaneous-Equation Model

Two-stage
least squares

$$I = -21.16 + 0.189X_1$$
$$(-2.96)\ (7.0)$$
$$+ 0.296I_{-1} + 0.518A_{-1}$$
$$(2.60) \qquad (3.6)$$
$$- 0.352A_{-2} - 0.125K_{-1}$$
$$(-2.07) \qquad (-4.2)$$
$$S = 4.091 \qquad d = 2.23$$

Limited-information
least squares

$$I = -19.11 + 0.176X_1$$
$$(-3.2) \quad (6.5)$$
$$+ 0.339I_{-1} - 0.540A_{-1}$$
$$(2.94) \qquad (3.7)$$
$$- 0.398A_{-2} - 0.118K_{-1}$$
$$(-2.32) \qquad (-3.9)$$
$$S = 4.126 \qquad d = 2.37$$

Labor, based on Equation (7-76):

Least squares

$$W = 3.46 + 0.487X_1$$
$$(3.1)\ (19.0)$$
$$+ 0.229W_{-1}$$
$$(5.3)$$
$$S = 1.938 \qquad R^2 = 0.999$$

Two-stage
least squares

$$W = 3.48 + 0.490X_1 +$$
$$(1.58)(18.8)$$
$$+ 0.223W_{-1}$$
$$(5.1)$$
$$S = 1.939 \qquad d = 1.61$$

Limited-information
least squares

$$W = 3.52 + 0.494X_1$$
$$(3.1)\ (18.9)$$
$$+ 0.216W_{-1}$$
$$(5.0)$$
$$S = 1.941 \qquad d = 1.57$$

Corporate saving, based on Equation (7-77):

Least squares

$$S = -4.64 + 0.468P$$
$$(-2.48)\ (8.0)$$
$$- 0.248P_{-1} + 0.450S_{-1}$$
$$(-3.1) \qquad (2.46)$$
$$S = 1.579 \qquad R^2 = 0.947$$

Simultaneous-Equation Model

Two-stage least squares

$$S = -4.89 + 0.488P$$
$$(-2.00)\ (7.7)$$

$$-0.257P_{-1} + 0.427S_{-1}$$
$$(-3.2) \qquad (2.31)$$

$$S = 1.584 \qquad d = 1.93$$

Limited-information least squares

$$S = -5.48 + 0.536P$$
$$(-2.79)\ (8.1)$$

$$-0.279P_{-1} + 0.374S_{-1}$$
$$(-3.3) \qquad (1.96)$$

$$S = 1.625 \qquad d = 1.96$$

Alternative investment, based on Equation (7-81):

Least squares

$$I = -7.61 + 0.107X_1$$
$$(-1.18)\ (3.0)$$

$$+ 0.613P + 0.266A_{-1}$$
$$(4.3) \qquad (2.27)$$

$$-0.275A_{-2} - 0.010K_{-1}$$
$$(-2.11) \qquad (-0.28)$$

$$S = 3.41 \qquad R^2 = 0.973$$

Two-stage least squares

$$I = -7.65 + 0.108X_1$$
$$(-1.02)\ (2.36)$$

$$+ 0.609P + 0.267A_{-1}$$
$$(3.8) \qquad (2.26)$$

$$-0.275A_{-2} - 0.011K_{-1}$$
$$(-2.11) \qquad (-0.28)$$

$$S = 3.41 \qquad d = 12.12$$

Limited-information least squares

$$I = -55.4 + 0.485X_1$$
$$(-1.42)(1.68)$$

$$-1.20P + 0.676A_{-1}$$
$$(-0.88) \quad (1.49)$$

$$-0.016A_{-2} - 0.317K_{-1}$$
$$(-0.04) \qquad (-1.30)$$

$$S = 10.07 \qquad d = 0.75$$

Several economic implications can be made based on Equations (7-74) through (7-81). The two-stage least-squares estimation of Equation (7-74) indicates that the marginal propensity to consume is 0.69. This value is the short-run propensity to consume. To get the long-run propensity, assuming that the long-run equilibrium $C_t =$

C_{t-1}, the value is estimated to be

$$\frac{0.686}{1 - 0.246} = 0.909, \qquad (7\text{-}82)$$

whereby 0.686 is the coefficient of Y and 0.246 is the coefficient of C_{-1}.

The investment equation, (7-75), suggests that the gross business product (X_1), the previous period of investment, and the stock prices in the preceding December have positive effects on the current investment. It can be argued that the higher stock prices indicate optimistic expectations for investment. Christ estimated 24 different investment equations, but many of them either have the wrong sign of the coefficients or the nonsignificant variables. Equation (7-75) is the one of the better two equations that he has chosen. Equation (7-81) is the alternative equation.

Labor equation (7-76) indicates that the real-labor income is positively affected by the gross business product and the lagged period real-labor income. The short-run propensity to use labor is 0.490, while the long-run propensity is 0.636 (0.490/(1 - 0.223)).

Finally, the estimated corporate saving, Equation (7-77), shows that real-property incomes and the previous corporate savings have positive effects on the corporate savings, but the previous period of the real-property incomes have negative effect on the corporate savings.

Interested students may consult Christ for further detailed discussions of the model.†

†*Ibid.*

APPENDIX A

Σ Notation

Summation notation Σ (also called sigma) is used extensively in this textbook. A review of certain basic summation rules would be helpful

$$\sum_{i=1}^{n} x_i = x_1 + x_2 + x_3 + \cdots + x_n \qquad \text{(A-1)}$$

Equation (A-1) means that the sum of x_i can be obtained by adding successive values of x_i, where i is equal to 1 through n.

$$\sum_{i=1}^{n} K x_i = K \sum_{i=1}^{n} x_i, \qquad \text{(A-2)}$$

where K is a constant.

$$\sum_{i=1}^{n} K = nK \qquad \text{(A-3)}$$

$$\sum_{i=1}^{n} (x_i + K) = \sum_{i=1}^{n} x_i + nK \qquad \text{(A-4)}$$

$$\sum_{i=1}^{n} x_i^2 = x_1^2 + x_2^2 + \cdots + x_n^2 \qquad \text{(A-5)}$$

$$\left(\sum_{i=1}^{n} x_i \right)^2 = (x_1 + x_2 + \cdots + x_n)^2$$

$$= x_1^2 + x_2^2 + \cdots + x_n^2 + 2x_1 x_2 + 2x_1 x_3 + \cdots$$

$$+ 2x_{n-1} x_n \qquad \text{(A-6)}$$

$$\sum_{i=1}^{n} (x_i + y_i) = \sum_{i=1}^{n} x_i + \sum_{i=1}^{n} y_i \qquad \text{(A-7)}$$

$$\sum_{i=1}^{n} x_i \sum_{i=1}^{n} y_i = (x_1 + x_2 + \cdots + x_n)(y_1 + y_2 + \cdots + y_n)$$

$$\text{(A-8)}$$

$$\sum_{i=1}^{n} x_i y_i = x_1 y_1 + x_2 y_2 + x_3 y_3 + \cdots + x_n y_n \quad \text{(A-9)}$$

$$\sum_{i=1}^{n} (x_i y_i)^2 = (x_1 y_1)^2 + (x_2 y_2)^2 + (x_3 y_3)^2 + \cdots + (x_n y_n)^2$$

$$\text{(A-10)}$$

$$\left(\sum_{i=1}^{n} x_i y_i\right)^2 = (x_1 y_1)^2 + (x_2 y_2)^2 + \cdots + (x_n y_n)^2$$

$$+ 2x_1 x_2 y_1 y_2 + 2x_1 x_3 y_1 y_3$$
$$+ \cdots + 2x_{n-1} x_n y_{n-1} y_n \quad \text{(A-11)}$$

The double summations are also used widely in this textbook. Following are some of the basic rules.

$$\sum_{i=1}^{n} \sum_{j=1}^{K} x_{ij} = \sum_{i=1}^{n} (x_{i1} + x_{i2}^2 + \cdots + x_{iK})$$

$$= x_{11} + x_{12} + \cdots + x_{1K} + x_{21} + x_{22} + \cdots$$
$$+ x_{2K} + \cdots + x_{nK} \quad \text{(A-12)}$$

$$\sum_{i=1}^{n} \sum_{j=1}^{K} x_i y_j = \sum_{i=1}^{n} (x_i y_1 + x_i y_2 + \cdots + x_i y_K)$$

$$= x_1 y_1 + x_1 y_2 + \cdots + x_1 y_K + x_2 y_1 + x_2 y_2$$
$$+ \cdots + x_2 y_K + \cdots + x_n y_K \quad \text{(A-13)}$$

$$\sum_{i=1}^{n} x_i \sum_{j=1}^{K} y_j = (x_1 + x_2 + \cdots + x_n)(y_1 + y_2 + \cdots + y_K)$$

$$= \sum_{i=1}^{n} \sum_{j=1}^{K} x_i y_j \quad \text{(A-14)}$$

$$\sum_{i=1}^{n} \sum_{j=1}^{K} (x_i + y_j)^2 = \sum_{i=1}^{n} x_i^2 + \sum_{j=1}^{K} y_j^2 + 2 \sum_{i=1}^{n} \sum_{j=1}^{K} x_i y_j$$

$$\text{(A-15)}$$

APPENDIX B

TABLE 1   The standardized normal distribution, $Z = \dfrac{X - \mu}{\sigma}$.

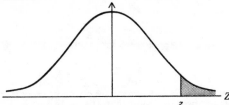

z	.00	.01	.02	.03	.04	.05	.06	.07	.08	.09
0.0	.5000	.4960	.4920	.4880	.4840	.4801	.4761	.4721	.4681	.4641
0.1	.4602	.4562	.4522	.4483	.4443	.4404	.4364	.4325	.4286	.4247
0.2	.4207	.4168	.4129	.4090	.4052	.4013	.3974	.3936	.3897	.3859
0.3	.3821	.3783	.3745	.3707	.3669	.3632	.3594	.3557	.3520	.3483
0.4	.3446	.3409	.3372	.3336	.3300	.3264	.3228	.3192	.3156	.3121
0.5	.3085	.3050	.3015	.2981	.2946	.2912	.2877	.2843	.2810	.2776
0.6	.2743	.2709	.2676	.2643	.2611	.2578	.2546	.2514	.2483	.2451
0.7	.2420	.2389	.2358	.2327	.2296	.2266	.2236	.2206	.2177	.2148
0.8	.2119	.2090	.2061	.2033	.2005	.1977	.1949	.1922	.1894	.1867
0.9	.1841	.1814	.1788	.1762	.1736	.1711	.1685	.1660	.1635	.1611
1.0	.1587	.1562	.1539	.1515	.1492	.1469	.1446	.1423	.1401	.1379
1.1	.1357	.1335	.1314	.1292	.1271	.1251	.1230	.1210	.1190	.1170
1.2	.1151	.1131	.1112	.1093	.1075	.1056	.1038	.1020	.1003	.0985
1.3	.0968	.0951	.0934	.0918	.0901	.0885	.0869	.0853	.0838	.0823
1.4	.0808	.0793	.0778	.0764	.0749	.0735	.0721	.0708	.0694	.0681
1.5	.0668	.0655	.0643	.0630	.0618	.0606	.0594	.0582	.0571	.0559
1.6	.0548	.0537	.0526	.0516	.0505	.0495	.0485	.0475	.0465	.0455
1.7	.0446	.0436	.0427	.0418	.0409	.0401	.0392	.0384	.0375	.0367
1.8	.0359	.0351	.0344	.0336	.0329	.0322	.0314	.0307	.0301	.0294
1.9	.0287	.0281	.0274	.0268	.0262	.0256	.0250	.0244	.0239	.0233
2.0	.0228	.0222	.0217	.0212	.0207	.0202	.0197	.0192	.0188	.0183
2.1	.0179	.0174	.0170	.0166	.0162	.0158	.0154	.0150	.0146	.0143
2.2	.0139	.0136	.0132	.0129	.0125	.0122	.0119	.0116	.0113	.0110
2.3	.0107	.0104	.0102	.0099	.0096	.0094	.0091	.0089	.0087	.0084
2.4	.0082	.0080	.0078	.0075	.0073	.0071	.0069	.0068	.0066	.0064
2.5	.0062	.0060	.0059	.0057	.0055	.0054	.0052	.0051	.0049	.0048
2.6	.0047	.0045	.0044	.0043	.0041	.0040	.0039	.0038	.0037	.0036
2.7	.0035	.0034	.0033	.0032	.0031	.0030	.0029	.0028	.0027	.0026
2.8	.0026	.0025	.0024	.0023	.0023	.0022	.0021	.0021	.0020	.0019
2.9	.0019	.0018	.0018	.0017	.0016	.0016	.0015	.0015	.0014	.0014
3.0	.0013	.0013	.0013	.0012	.0012	.0011	.0011	.0011	.0010	.0010

The table plots the cumulative probability $Z \geqslant z$.

TABLE 2 Student's t Distribution.

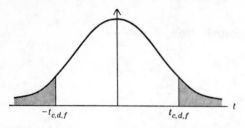

Degrees of freedom	Probability of a value greater in absolute value than the table entry					
	0.005	0.01	0.025	0.05	0.1	0.15
1	63.657	31.821	12.706	6.314	3.078	1.963
2	9.925	6.965	4.303	2.920	1.886	1.386
3	5.841	4.541	3.182	2.353	1.638	1.250
4	4.604	3.747	2.776	2.132	1.533	1.190
5	4.032	3.365	2.571	2.015	1.476	1.156
6	3.707	3.143	2.447	1.943	1.440	1.134
7	3.499	2.998	2.365	1.895	1.415	1.119
8	3.355	2.896	2.306	1.860	1.397	1.108
9	3.250	2.821	2.262	1.833	1.383	1.100
10	3.169	2.764	2.228	1.812	1.372	1.093
11	3.106	2.718	2.201	1.796	1.363	1.088
12	3.055	2.681	2.179	1.782	1.356	1.083
13	3.012	2.650	2.160	1.771	1.350	1.079
14	2.977	2.624	2.145	1.761	1.345	1.076
15	2.947	2.602	2.131	1.753	1.341	1.074
16	2.921	2.583	2.120	1.746	1.337	1.071
17	2.898	2.567	2.110	1.740	1.333	1.069
18	2.878	2.552	2.101	1.734	1.330	1.067
19	2.861	2.539	2.093	1.729	1.328	1.066
20	2.845	2.528	2.086	1.725	1.325	1.064
21	2.831	2.518	2.080	1.721	1.323	1.063
22	2.819	2.508	2.074	1.717	1.321	1.061
23	2.807	2.500	2.069	1.714	1.319	1.060
24	2.797	2.492	2.064	1.711	1.318	1.059
25	2.787	2.485	2.060	1.708	1.316	1.058
26	2.779	2.479	2.056	1.706	1.315	1.058
27	2.771	2.473	2.052	1.703	1.314	1.057
28	2.763	2.467	2.048	1.701	1.313	1.056
29	2.756	2.462	2.045	1.699	1.311	1.055
30	2.750	2.457	2.042	1.697	1.310	1.055
∞	2.576	2.326	1.960	1.645	1.282	1.036

SOURCE: Reprinted from Table IV in Sir Ronald A. Fisher, *Statistical Methods for Research Workers*, 13th edition (Edinburgh, Oliver & Boyd Ltd., 1963), with the permission of the publisher and the late Sir Ronald Fisher's Literary Executor.

TABLE 3 Critical values for the F distribution.

5% (Roman Type) and 1% (Bold Face Type) Points for the Distribution of F.

$f(F; n_1, n_2)$

Each cell shows the 5% point (Roman) and the 1% point (bold).

n_1, degrees of freedom in the numerator

n_2	1	2	3	4	5	6	7	8	9	10	11	12	14	16	20	24	30	40	50	75	100	200	500	∞
1	161 / **4,052**	200 / **4,999**	216 / **5,403**	225 / **5,625**	230 / **5,764**	234 / **5,859**	237 / **5,928**	239 / **5,981**	241 / **6,022**	242 / **6,056**	243 / **6,082**	244 / **6,106**	245 / **6,142**	246 / **6,169**	248 / **6,208**	249 / **6,234**	250 / **6,258**	251 / **6,286**	252 / **6,302**	253 / **6,323**	253 / **6,334**	254 / **6,352**	254 / **6,361**	254 / **6,366**
2	18.51 / **98.49**	19.00 / **99.00**	19.16 / **99.17**	19.25 / **99.25**	19.30 / **99.30**	19.33 / **99.33**	19.36 / **99.34**	19.37 / **99.36**	19.38 / **99.38**	19.39 / **99.40**	19.40 / **99.41**	19.41 / **99.42**	19.42 / **99.43**	19.43 / **99.44**	19.44 / **99.45**	19.45 / **99.46**	19.46 / **99.47**	19.47 / **99.48**	19.47 / **99.48**	19.48 / **99.49**	19.49 / **99.49**	19.49 / **99.49**	19.50 / **99.50**	19.50 / **99.50**
3	10.13 / **34.12**	9.55 / **30.82**	9.28 / **29.46**	9.12 / **28.71**	9.01 / **28.24**	8.94 / **27.91**	8.88 / **27.67**	8.84 / **27.49**	8.81 / **27.34**	8.78 / **27.23**	8.76 / **27.13**	8.74 / **27.05**	8.71 / **26.92**	8.69 / **26.83**	8.66 / **26.69**	8.64 / **26.60**	8.62 / **26.50**	8.60 / **26.41**	8.58 / **26.35**	8.57 / **26.27**	8.56 / **26.23**	8.54 / **26.18**	8.54 / **26.14**	8.53 / **26.12**
4	7.71 / **21.20**	6.94 / **18.00**	6.59 / **16.69**	6.39 / **15.98**	6.26 / **15.52**	6.16 / **15.21**	6.09 / **14.98**	6.04 / **14.80**	6.00 / **14.66**	5.96 / **14.54**	5.93 / **14.45**	5.91 / **14.37**	5.87 / **14.24**	5.84 / **14.15**	5.80 / **14.02**	5.77 / **13.93**	5.74 / **13.83**	5.71 / **13.74**	5.70 / **13.69**	5.68 / **13.61**	5.66 / **13.57**	5.65 / **13.52**	5.64 / **13.48**	5.63 / **13.46**
5	6.61 / **16.26**	5.79 / **13.27**	5.41 / **12.06**	5.19 / **11.39**	5.05 / **10.97**	4.95 / **10.67**	4.88 / **10.45**	4.82 / **10.27**	4.78 / **10.15**	4.74 / **10.05**	4.70 / **9.96**	4.68 / **9.89**	4.64 / **9.77**	4.60 / **9.68**	4.56 / **9.55**	4.53 / **9.47**	4.50 / **9.38**	4.46 / **9.29**	4.44 / **9.24**	4.42 / **9.17**	4.40 / **9.13**	4.38 / **9.07**	4.37 / **9.04**	4.36 / **9.02**
6	5.99 / **13.74**	5.14 / **10.92**	4.76 / **9.78**	4.53 / **9.15**	4.39 / **8.75**	4.28 / **8.47**	4.21 / **8.26**	4.15 / **8.10**	4.10 / **7.98**	4.06 / **7.87**	4.03 / **7.79**	4.00 / **7.72**	3.96 / **7.60**	3.92 / **7.52**	3.87 / **7.39**	3.84 / **7.31**	3.81 / **7.23**	3.77 / **7.14**	3.75 / **7.09**	3.72 / **7.02**	3.71 / **6.99**	3.69 / **6.94**	3.68 / **6.90**	3.67 / **6.88**
7	5.59 / **12.25**	4.74 / **9.55**	4.35 / **8.45**	4.12 / **7.85**	3.97 / **7.46**	3.87 / **7.19**	3.79 / **7.00**	3.73 / **6.84**	3.68 / **6.71**	3.63 / **6.62**	3.60 / **6.54**	3.57 / **6.47**	3.52 / **6.35**	3.49 / **6.27**	3.44 / **6.15**	3.41 / **6.07**	3.38 / **5.98**	3.34 / **5.90**	3.32 / **5.85**	3.29 / **5.78**	3.28 / **5.75**	3.25 / **5.70**	3.24 / **5.67**	3.23 / **5.65**
8	5.32 / **11.26**	4.46 / **8.65**	4.07 / **7.59**	3.84 / **7.01**	3.69 / **6.63**	3.58 / **6.37**	3.50 / **6.19**	3.44 / **6.03**	3.39 / **5.91**	3.34 / **5.82**	3.31 / **5.74**	3.28 / **5.67**	3.23 / **5.56**	3.20 / **5.48**	3.15 / **5.36**	3.12 / **5.28**	3.08 / **5.20**	3.05 / **5.11**	3.03 / **5.06**	3.00 / **5.00**	2.98 / **4.96**	2.96 / **4.91**	2.94 / **4.88**	2.93 / **4.86**
9	5.12 / **10.56**	4.26 / **8.02**	3.86 / **6.99**	3.63 / **6.42**	3.48 / **6.06**	3.37 / **5.80**	3.29 / **5.62**	3.23 / **5.47**	3.18 / **5.35**	3.13 / **5.26**	3.10 / **5.18**	3.07 / **5.11**	3.02 / **5.00**	2.98 / **4.92**	2.93 / **4.80**	2.90 / **4.73**	2.86 / **4.64**	2.82 / **4.56**	2.80 / **4.51**	2.77 / **4.45**	2.76 / **4.41**	2.73 / **4.36**	2.72 / **4.33**	2.71 / **4.31**
10	4.96 / **10.04**	4.10 / **7.56**	3.71 / **6.55**	3.48 / **5.99**	3.33 / **5.64**	3.22 / **5.39**	3.14 / **5.21**	3.07 / **5.06**	3.02 / **4.95**	2.97 / **4.85**	2.94 / **4.78**	2.91 / **4.71**	2.86 / **4.60**	2.82 / **4.52**	2.77 / **4.41**	2.74 / **4.33**	2.70 / **4.25**	2.67 / **4.17**	2.64 / **4.12**	2.61 / **4.05**	2.59 / **4.01**	2.56 / **3.96**	2.55 / **3.93**	2.54 / **3.91**
11	4.84 / **9.65**	3.98 / **7.20**	3.59 / **6.22**	3.36 / **5.67**	3.20 / **5.32**	3.09 / **5.07**	3.01 / **4.88**	2.95 / **4.74**	2.90 / **4.63**	2.86 / **4.54**	2.82 / **4.46**	2.79 / **4.40**	2.74 / **4.29**	2.70 / **4.21**	2.65 / **4.10**	2.61 / **4.02**	2.57 / **3.94**	2.53 / **3.86**	2.50 / **3.80**	2.47 / **3.74**	2.45 / **3.70**	2.42 / **3.66**	2.41 / **3.62**	2.40 / **3.60**
12	4.75 / **9.33**	3.88 / **6.93**	3.49 / **5.95**	3.26 / **5.41**	3.11 / **5.06**	3.00 / **4.82**	2.92 / **4.65**	2.85 / **4.50**	2.80 / **4.39**	2.76 / **4.30**	2.72 / **4.22**	2.69 / **4.16**	2.64 / **4.05**	2.60 / **3.98**	2.54 / **3.86**	2.50 / **3.78**	2.46 / **3.70**	2.42 / **3.61**	2.40 / **3.56**	2.36 / **3.49**	2.35 / **3.46**	2.32 / **3.41**	2.31 / **3.38**	2.30 / **3.36**
13	4.67 / **9.07**	3.80 / **6.70**	3.41 / **5.74**	3.18 / **5.20**	3.02 / **4.86**	2.92 / **4.62**	2.84 / **4.44**	2.77 / **4.30**	2.72 / **4.19**	2.67 / **4.10**	2.63 / **4.02**	2.60 / **3.96**	2.55 / **3.85**	2.51 / **3.78**	2.46 / **3.67**	2.42 / **3.59**	2.38 / **3.51**	2.34 / **3.42**	2.32 / **3.37**	2.28 / **3.30**	2.26 / **3.27**	2.24 / **3.21**	2.22 / **3.18**	2.21 / **3.16**

Reprinted by permission from Statistical Methods, 5th edition, by George W. Snedecor, © 1956 by The Iowa State University Press, Ames, Iowa.

TABLE 3 (continued)

n_1, degrees of freedom (for greater mean square)

n_2	1	2	3	4	5	6	7	8	9	10	11	12	14	16	20	24	30	40	50	75	100	200	500	∞
14	4.60 / 8.86	3.74 / 6.51	3.34 / 5.56	3.11 / 5.03	2.96 / 4.69	2.85 / 4.46	2.77 / 4.28	2.70 / 4.14	2.65 / 4.03	2.60 / 3.94	2.56 / 3.86	2.53 / 3.80	2.48 / 3.70	2.44 / 3.62	2.39 / 3.51	2.35 / 3.43	2.31 / 3.34	2.27 / 3.26	2.24 / 3.21	2.21 / 3.14	2.19 / 3.11	2.16 / 3.06	2.14 / 3.02	2.13 / 3.00
15	4.54 / 8.68	3.68 / 6.36	3.29 / 5.42	3.06 / 4.89	2.90 / 4.56	2.79 / 4.32	2.70 / 4.14	2.64 / 4.00	2.59 / 3.89	2.55 / 3.80	2.51 / 3.73	2.48 / 3.67	2.43 / 3.56	2.39 / 3.48	2.33 / 3.36	2.29 / 3.29	2.25 / 3.20	2.21 / 3.12	2.18 / 3.07	2.15 / 3.00	2.12 / 2.97	2.10 / 2.92	2.08 / 2.89	2.07 / 2.87
16	4.49 / 8.53	3.63 / 6.23	3.24 / 5.29	3.01 / 4.77	2.85 / 4.44	2.74 / 4.20	2.66 / 4.03	2.59 / 3.89	2.54 / 3.78	2.49 / 3.69	2.45 / 3.61	2.42 / 3.55	2.37 / 3.45	2.33 / 3.37	2.28 / 3.25	2.24 / 3.18	2.20 / 3.10	2.16 / 3.01	2.13 / 2.96	2.09 / 2.89	2.07 / 2.86	2.04 / 2.80	2.02 / 2.77	2.01 / 2.75
17	4.45 / 8.40	3.59 / 6.11	3.20 / 5.18	2.96 / 4.67	2.81 / 4.34	2.70 / 4.10	2.62 / 3.93	2.55 / 3.79	2.50 / 3.68	2.45 / 3.59	2.41 / 3.52	2.38 / 3.45	2.33 / 3.35	2.29 / 3.27	2.23 / 3.16	2.19 / 3.08	2.15 / 3.00	2.11 / 2.92	2.08 / 2.86	2.04 / 2.79	2.02 / 2.76	1.99 / 2.70	1.97 / 2.67	1.96 / 2.65
18	4.41 / 8.28	3.55 / 6.01	3.16 / 5.09	2.93 / 4.58	2.77 / 4.25	2.66 / 4.01	2.58 / 3.85	2.51 / 3.71	2.46 / 3.60	2.41 / 3.51	2.37 / 3.44	2.34 / 3.37	2.29 / 3.27	2.25 / 3.19	2.19 / 3.07	2.15 / 3.00	2.11 / 2.91	2.07 / 2.83	2.04 / 2.78	2.00 / 2.71	1.98 / 2.68	1.95 / 2.62	1.93 / 2.59	1.92 / 2.57
19	4.38 / 8.18	3.52 / 5.93	3.13 / 5.01	2.90 / 4.50	2.74 / 4.17	2.63 / 3.94	2.55 / 3.77	2.48 / 3.63	2.43 / 3.52	2.38 / 3.43	2.34 / 3.36	2.31 / 3.30	2.26 / 3.19	2.21 / 3.12	2.15 / 3.00	2.11 / 2.92	2.07 / 2.84	2.02 / 2.76	2.00 / 2.70	1.96 / 2.63	1.94 / 2.60	1.91 / 2.54	1.90 / 2.51	1.88 / 2.49
20	4.35 / 8.10	3.49 / 5.85	3.10 / 4.94	2.87 / 4.43	2.71 / 4.10	2.60 / 3.87	2.52 / 3.71	2.45 / 3.56	2.40 / 3.45	2.35 / 3.37	2.31 / 3.30	2.28 / 3.23	2.23 / 3.13	2.18 / 3.05	2.12 / 2.94	2.08 / 2.86	2.04 / 2.77	1.99 / 2.69	1.96 / 2.63	1.92 / 2.56	1.90 / 2.53	1.87 / 2.47	1.85 / 2.44	1.84 / 2.42
21	4.32 / 8.02	3.47 / 5.78	3.07 / 4.87	2.84 / 4.37	2.68 / 4.04	2.57 / 3.81	2.49 / 3.65	2.42 / 3.51	2.37 / 3.40	2.32 / 3.31	2.28 / 3.24	2.25 / 3.17	2.20 / 3.07	2.15 / 2.99	2.09 / 2.88	2.05 / 2.80	2.00 / 2.72	1.96 / 2.63	1.93 / 2.58	1.89 / 2.51	1.87 / 2.47	1.84 / 2.42	1.82 / 2.38	1.81 / 2.36
22	4.30 / 7.94	3.44 / 5.72	3.05 / 4.82	2.82 / 4.31	2.66 / 3.99	2.55 / 3.76	2.47 / 3.59	2.40 / 3.45	2.35 / 3.35	2.30 / 3.26	2.26 / 3.18	2.23 / 3.12	2.18 / 3.02	2.13 / 2.94	2.07 / 2.83	2.03 / 2.75	1.98 / 2.67	1.93 / 2.58	1.91 / 2.53	1.87 / 2.46	1.84 / 2.42	1.81 / 2.37	1.80 / 2.33	1.78 / 2.31
23	4.28 / 7.88	3.42 / 5.66	3.03 / 4.76	2.80 / 4.26	2.64 / 3.94	2.53 / 3.71	2.45 / 3.54	2.38 / 3.41	2.32 / 3.30	2.28 / 3.21	2.24 / 3.14	2.20 / 3.07	2.14 / 2.97	2.10 / 2.89	2.04 / 2.78	2.00 / 2.70	1.96 / 2.62	1.91 / 2.53	1.88 / 2.48	1.84 / 2.41	1.82 / 2.37	1.79 / 2.32	1.77 / 2.28	1.76 / 2.26
24	4.26 / 7.82	3.40 / 5.61	3.01 / 4.72	2.78 / 4.22	2.62 / 3.90	2.51 / 3.67	2.43 / 3.50	2.36 / 3.36	2.30 / 3.25	2.26 / 3.17	2.22 / 3.09	2.18 / 3.03	2.13 / 2.93	2.09 / 2.85	2.02 / 2.74	1.98 / 2.66	1.94 / 2.58	1.89 / 2.49	1.86 / 2.44	1.82 / 2.36	1.80 / 2.33	1.76 / 2.27	1.74 / 2.23	1.73 / 2.21
25	4.24 / 7.77	3.38 / 5.57	2.99 / 4.68	2.76 / 4.18	2.60 / 3.86	2.49 / 3.63	2.41 / 3.46	2.34 / 3.32	2.28 / 3.21	2.24 / 3.13	2.20 / 3.05	2.16 / 2.99	2.11 / 2.89	2.06 / 2.81	2.00 / 2.70	1.96 / 2.62	1.92 / 2.54	1.87 / 2.45	1.84 / 2.40	1.80 / 2.32	1.77 / 2.29	1.74 / 2.23	1.72 / 2.19	1.71 / 2.17
26	4.22 / 7.72	3.37 / 5.53	2.98 / 4.64	2.74 / 4.14	2.59 / 3.82	2.47 / 3.59	2.39 / 3.42	2.32 / 3.29	2.27 / 3.17	2.22 / 3.09	2.18 / 3.02	2.15 / 2.96	2.10 / 2.86	2.05 / 2.77	1.99 / 2.66	1.95 / 2.58	1.90 / 2.50	1.85 / 2.41	1.82 / 2.36	1.78 / 2.28	1.76 / 2.25	1.72 / 2.19	1.70 / 2.15	1.69 / 2.13

TABLE 3 (continued)

n_1 degrees of freedom (for greater mean square)

n_2	1	2	3	4	5	6	7	8	9	10	11	12	14	16	20	24	30	40	50	75	100	200	500	∞	n_2
27	4.21 7.68	3.35 5.49	2.96 4.60	2.73 4.11	2.57 3.79	2.46 3.56	2.37 3.39	2.30 3.26	2.25 3.14	2.20 3.06	2.16 2.98	2.13 2.93	2.08 2.83	2.03 2.74	1.97 2.63	1.93 2.55	1.88 2.47	1.84 2.38	1.80 2.33	1.76 2.25	1.74 2.21	1.71 2.16	1.68 2.12	1.67 2.10	27
28	4.20 7.64	3.34 5.45	2.95 4.57	2.71 4.07	2.56 3.76	2.44 3.53	2.36 3.36	2.29 3.23	2.24 3.11	2.19 3.03	2.15 2.95	2.12 2.90	2.06 2.80	2.02 2.71	1.96 2.60	1.91 2.52	1.87 2.44	1.81 2.35	1.78 2.30	1.75 2.22	1.72 2.18	1.69 2.13	1.67 2.09	1.65 2.06	28
29	4.18 7.60	3.33 5.42	2.93 4.54	2.70 4.04	2.54 3.73	2.43 3.50	2.35 3.33	2.28 3.20	2.22 3.08	2.18 3.00	2.14 2.92	2.10 2.87	2.05 2.77	2.00 2.68	1.94 2.57	1.90 2.49	1.85 2.41	1.80 2.32	1.77 2.27	1.73 2.19	1.71 2.15	1.68 2.10	1.65 2.06	1.64 2.03	29
30	4.17 7.56	3.32 5.39	2.92 4.51	2.69 4.02	2.53 3.70	2.42 3.47	2.34 3.30	2.27 3.17	2.21 3.06	2.16 2.98	2.12 2.90	2.09 2.84	2.04 2.74	1.99 2.66	1.93 2.55	1.89 2.47	1.84 2.38	1.79 2.29	1.76 2.24	1.72 2.16	1.69 2.13	1.66 2.07	1.64 2.03	1.62 2.01	30
32	4.15 7.50	3.30 5.34	2.90 4.46	2.67 3.97	2.51 3.66	2.40 3.42	2.32 3.25	2.25 3.12	2.19 3.01	2.14 2.94	2.10 2.86	2.07 2.80	2.02 2.70	1.97 2.62	1.91 2.51	1.86 2.42	1.82 2.34	1.76 2.25	1.74 2.20	1.69 2.12	1.67 2.08	1.64 2.02	1.61 1.98	1.59 1.96	32
34	4.13 7.44	3.28 5.29	2.88 4.42	2.65 3.93	2.49 3.61	2.38 3.38	2.30 3.21	2.23 3.08	2.17 2.97	2.12 2.89	2.08 2.82	2.05 2.76	2.00 2.66	1.95 2.58	1.89 2.47	1.84 2.38	1.80 2.30	1.74 2.21	1.71 2.15	1.67 2.08	1.64 2.04	1.61 1.98	1.59 1.94	1.57 1.91	34
36	4.11 7.39	3.26 5.25	2.86 4.38	2.63 3.89	2.48 3.58	2.36 3.35	2.28 3.18	2.21 3.04	2.15 2.94	2.10 2.86	2.06 2.78	2.03 2.72	1.98 2.62	1.93 2.54	1.87 2.43	1.82 2.35	1.78 2.26	1.72 2.17	1.69 2.12	1.65 2.04	1.62 2.00	1.59 1.94	1.56 1.90	1.55 1.87	36
38	4.10 7.35	3.25 5.21	2.85 4.34	2.62 3.86	2.46 3.54	2.35 3.32	2.26 3.15	2.19 3.02	2.14 2.91	2.09 2.82	2.05 2.75	2.02 2.69	1.96 2.59	1.92 2.51	1.85 2.40	1.80 2.32	1.76 2.22	1.71 2.14	1.67 2.08	1.63 2.00	1.60 1.97	1.57 1.90	1.54 1.86	1.53 1.84	38
40	4.08 7.31	3.23 5.18	2.84 4.31	2.61 3.83	2.45 3.51	2.34 3.29	2.25 3.12	2.18 2.99	2.12 2.88	2.07 2.80	2.04 2.73	2.00 2.66	1.95 2.56	1.90 2.49	1.84 2.37	1.79 2.29	1.74 2.20	1.69 2.11	1.66 2.05	1.61 1.97	1.59 1.94	1.55 1.88	1.53 1.84	1.51 1.81	40
42	4.07 7.27	3.22 5.15	2.83 4.29	2.59 3.80	2.44 3.49	2.32 3.26	2.24 3.10	2.17 2.96	2.11 2.86	2.06 2.77	2.02 2.70	1.99 2.64	1.94 2.54	1.89 2.46	1.82 2.35	1.78 2.26	1.73 2.17	1.68 2.08	1.64 2.02	1.60 1.94	1.57 1.91	1.54 1.85	1.51 1.80	1.49 1.78	42
44	4.06 7.24	3.21 5.12	2.82 4.26	2.58 3.78	2.43 3.46	2.31 3.24	2.23 3.07	2.16 2.94	2.10 2.84	2.05 2.75	2.01 2.68	1.98 2.62	1.92 2.52	1.88 2.44	1.81 2.32	1.76 2.24	1.72 2.15	1.66 2.06	1.63 2.00	1.58 1.92	1.56 1.88	1.52 1.82	1.50 1.78	1.48 1.75	44
46	4.05 7.21	3.20 5.10	2.81 4.24	2.57 3.76	2.42 3.44	2.30 3.22	2.22 3.05	2.14 2.92	2.09 2.82	2.04 2.73	2.00 2.66	1.97 2.60	1.91 2.50	1.87 2.42	1.80 2.30	1.75 2.22	1.71 2.13	1.65 2.04	1.62 1.98	1.57 1.90	1.54 1.86	1.51 1.80	1.48 1.76	1.46 1.72	46
48	4.04 7.19	3.19 5.08	2.80 4.22	2.56 3.74	2.41 3.42	2.30 3.20	2.21 3.04	2.14 2.90	2.08 2.80	2.03 2.71	1.99 2.64	1.96 2.58	1.90 2.48	1.86 2.40	1.79 2.28	1.74 2.20	1.70 2.11	1.64 2.02	1.61 1.96	1.56 1.88	1.53 1.84	1.50 1.78	1.47 1.73	1.45 1.70	48

TABLE 3 (continued)

SOURCE: George W. Snedecor, *Statistical Methods*, 5th edition, 1956, pp. 246–249. The Iowa State University Press, Ames, Iowa: The Iowa State University Press. Copyright © 1956 by the Iowa State University Press: reprinted by permission. The function $F = e$ with exponent $2z$, is computed in part from Fisher's table VI(7). Additional entries are by interpolation, mostly graphical.

Each cell lists two values: the upper (light) and lower (bold) entry.

n_1, degrees of freedom (for greater mean square)

n_2	1	2	3	4	5	6	7	8	9	10	11	12	14	16	20	24	30	40	50	75	100	200	500	∞	n_2
50	4.03 / 7.17	3.18 / 5.06	2.79 / 4.20	2.56 / 3.72	2.40 / 3.41	2.29 / 3.18	2.20 / 3.02	2.13 / 2.88	2.07 / 2.78	2.02 / 2.70	1.98 / 2.62	1.95 / 2.56	1.90 / 2.46	1.85 / 2.39	1.78 / 2.26	1.74 / 2.18	1.69 / 2.10	1.63 / 2.00	1.60 / 1.94	1.55 / 1.86	1.52 / 1.82	1.48 / 1.76	1.46 / 1.71	1.44 / 1.68	50
55	4.02 / 7.12	3.17 / 5.01	2.78 / 4.16	2.54 / 3.68	2.38 / 3.37	2.27 / 3.15	2.18 / 2.98	2.11 / 2.85	2.05 / 2.75	2.00 / 2.66	1.97 / 2.59	1.93 / 2.53	1.88 / 2.43	1.83 / 2.35	1.76 / 2.23	1.72 / 2.15	1.67 / 2.06	1.61 / 1.96	1.58 / 1.90	1.52 / 1.82	1.50 / 1.78	1.46 / 1.71	1.43 / 1.66	1.41 / 1.64	55
60	4.00 / 7.08	3.15 / 4.98	2.76 / 4.13	2.52 / 3.65	2.37 / 3.34	2.25 / 3.12	2.17 / 2.95	2.10 / 2.82	2.04 / 2.72	1.99 / 2.63	1.95 / 2.56	1.92 / 2.50	1.86 / 2.40	1.81 / 2.32	1.75 / 2.20	1.70 / 2.12	1.65 / 2.03	1.59 / 1.93	1.56 / 1.87	1.50 / 1.79	1.48 / 1.74	1.44 / 1.68	1.41 / 1.63	1.39 / 1.60	60
65	3.99 / 7.04	3.14 / 4.95	2.75 / 4.10	2.51 / 3.62	2.36 / 3.31	2.24 / 3.09	2.15 / 2.93	2.08 / 2.79	2.02 / 2.70	1.98 / 2.61	1.94 / 2.54	1.90 / 2.47	1.85 / 2.37	1.80 / 2.30	1.73 / 2.18	1.68 / 2.09	1.63 / 2.00	1.57 / 1.90	1.54 / 1.84	1.49 / 1.76	1.46 / 1.71	1.42 / 1.64	1.39 / 1.60	1.37 / 1.56	65
70	3.98 / 7.01	3.13 / 4.92	2.74 / 4.08	2.50 / 3.60	2.35 / 3.29	2.23 / 3.07	2.14 / 2.91	2.07 / 2.77	2.01 / 2.67	1.97 / 2.59	1.93 / 2.51	1.89 / 2.45	1.84 / 2.35	1.79 / 2.28	1.72 / 2.15	1.67 / 2.07	1.62 / 1.98	1.56 / 1.88	1.53 / 1.82	1.47 / 1.74	1.45 / 1.69	1.40 / 1.62	1.37 / 1.56	1.35 / 1.53	70
80	3.96 / 6.96	3.11 / 4.88	2.72 / 4.04	2.48 / 3.56	2.33 / 3.25	2.21 / 3.04	2.12 / 2.87	2.05 / 2.74	1.99 / 2.64	1.95 / 2.55	1.91 / 2.48	1.88 / 2.41	1.82 / 2.32	1.77 / 2.24	1.70 / 2.11	1.65 / 2.03	1.60 / 1.94	1.54 / 1.84	1.51 / 1.78	1.45 / 1.70	1.42 / 1.65	1.38 / 1.57	1.35 / 1.52	1.32 / 1.49	80
100	3.94 / 6.90	3.09 / 4.82	2.70 / 3.98	2.46 / 3.51	2.30 / 3.20	2.19 / 2.99	2.10 / 2.82	2.03 / 2.69	1.97 / 2.59	1.92 / 2.51	1.88 / 2.43	1.85 / 2.36	1.79 / 2.26	1.75 / 2.19	1.68 / 2.06	1.63 / 1.98	1.57 / 1.89	1.51 / 1.79	1.48 / 1.73	1.42 / 1.64	1.39 / 1.59	1.34 / 1.51	1.30 / 1.46	1.28 / 1.43	100
125	3.92 / 6.84	3.07 / 4.78	2.68 / 3.94	2.44 / 3.47	2.29 / 3.17	2.17 / 2.95	2.08 / 2.79	2.01 / 2.65	1.95 / 2.56	1.90 / 2.47	1.86 / 2.40	1.83 / 2.33	1.77 / 2.23	1.72 / 2.15	1.65 / 2.03	1.60 / 1.94	1.55 / 1.85	1.49 / 1.75	1.45 / 1.68	1.39 / 1.59	1.36 / 1.54	1.31 / 1.46	1.27 / 1.40	1.25 / 1.37	125
150	3.91 / 6.81	3.06 / 4.75	2.67 / 3.91	2.43 / 3.44	2.27 / 3.14	2.16 / 2.92	2.07 / 2.76	2.00 / 2.62	1.94 / 2.53	1.89 / 2.44	1.85 / 2.37	1.82 / 2.30	1.76 / 2.20	1.71 / 2.12	1.64 / 2.00	1.59 / 1.91	1.54 / 1.83	1.47 / 1.72	1.44 / 1.66	1.37 / 1.56	1.34 / 1.51	1.29 / 1.43	1.25 / 1.37	1.22 / 1.33	150
200	3.89 / 6.76	3.04 / 4.71	2.65 / 3.88	2.41 / 3.41	2.26 / 3.11	2.14 / 2.90	2.05 / 2.73	1.98 / 2.60	1.92 / 2.50	1.87 / 2.41	1.83 / 2.34	1.80 / 2.28	1.74 / 2.17	1.69 / 2.09	1.62 / 1.97	1.57 / 1.88	1.52 / 1.79	1.45 / 1.69	1.42 / 1.62	1.35 / 1.53	1.32 / 1.48	1.26 / 1.39	1.22 / 1.33	1.19 / 1.28	200
400	3.86 / 6.70	3.02 / 4.66	2.62 / 3.83	2.39 / 3.36	2.23 / 3.06	2.12 / 2.85	2.03 / 2.69	1.96 / 2.55	1.90 / 2.46	1.85 / 2.37	1.81 / 2.29	1.78 / 2.23	1.72 / 2.12	1.67 / 2.04	1.60 / 1.92	1.54 / 1.84	1.49 / 1.74	1.42 / 1.64	1.38 / 1.57	1.32 / 1.47	1.28 / 1.42	1.22 / 1.32	1.16 / 1.24	1.13 / 1.19	400
1000	3.85 / 6.66	3.00 / 4.62	2.61 / 3.80	2.38 / 3.34	2.22 / 3.04	2.10 / 2.82	2.02 / 2.66	1.95 / 2.53	1.89 / 2.43	1.84 / 2.34	1.80 / 2.26	1.76 / 2.20	1.70 / 2.09	1.65 / 2.01	1.58 / 1.89	1.53 / 1.81	1.47 / 1.71	1.41 / 1.61	1.36 / 1.54	1.30 / 1.44	1.26 / 1.38	1.19 / 1.28	1.13 / 1.19	1.08 / 1.11	1000
∞	3.84 / 6.64	2.99 / 4.60	2.60 / 3.78	2.37 / 3.32	2.21 / 3.02	2.09 / 2.80	2.01 / 2.64	1.94 / 2.51	1.88 / 2.41	1.83 / 2.32	1.79 / 2.24	1.75 / 2.18	1.69 / 2.07	1.64 / 1.99	1.57 / 1.87	1.52 / 1.79	1.46 / 1.69	1.40 / 1.59	1.35 / 1.52	1.28 / 1.41	1.24 / 1.36	1.17 / 1.25	1.11 / 1.15	1.00 / 1.00	∞

TABLE 4 Critical values for the Durbin-Watson test; 5% significance points of d_l and d_u in two-tailed tests.

n	$k' = 1$		$k' = 2$		$k' = 3$		$k' = 4$		$k' = 5$	
	d_l	d_u	d_l	d_u	d_l	d_u	d_l	d_u	d_l	d_u
15	0.95	1.23	0.83	1.40	0.71	1.61	0.59	1.84	0.48	2.09
16	0.98	1.24	0.86	1.40	0.75	1.59	0.64	1.80	0.53	2.03
17	1.01	1.25	0.90	1.40	0.79	1.58	0.68	1.77	0.57	1.98
18	1.03	1.26	0.93	1.40	0.82	1.56	0.72	1.74	0.62	1.93
19	1.06	1.28	0.96	1.41	0.86	1.55	0.76	1.72	0.66	1.90
20	1.08	1.28	0.99	1.41	0.89	1.55	0.79	1.70	0.70	1.87
21	1.10	1.30	1.01	1.41	0.92	1.54	0.83	1.69	0.73	1.84
22	1.12	1.31	1.04	1.42	0.95	1.54	0.86	1.68	0.77	1.82
23	1.14	1.32	1.06	1.42	0.97	1.54	0.89	1.67	0.80	1.80
24	1.16	1.33	1.08	1.43	1.00	1.54	0.91	1.66	0.83	1.79
25	1.18	1.34	1.10	1.43	1.02	1.54	0.94	1.65	0.86	1.77
26	1.19	1.35	1.12	1.44	1.04	1.54	0.96	1.65	0.88	1.76
27	1.21	1.36	1.13	1.44	1.06	1.54	0.99	1.64	0.91	1.75
28	1.22	1.37	1.15	1.45	1.08	1.54	1.01	1.64	0.93	1.74
29	1.24	1.38	1.17	1.45	1.10	1.54	1.03	1.63	0.96	1.73
30	1.25	1.38	1.18	1.46	1.12	1.54	1.05	1.63	0.98	1.73
31	1.26	1.39	1.20	1.47	1.13	1.55	1.07	1.63	1.00	1.72
32	1.27	1.40	1.21	1.47	1.15	1.55	1.08	1.63	1.02	1.71
33	1.28	1.41	1.22	1.48	1.16	1.55	1.10	1.63	1.04	1.71
34	1.29	1.41	1.24	1.48	1.17	1.55	1.12	1.63	1.06	1.70
35	1.30	1.42	1.25	1.48	1.19	1.55	1.13	1.63	1.07	1.70
36	1.31	1.43	1.26	1.49	1.20	1.56	1.15	1.63	1.09	1.70
37	1.32	1.43	1.27	1.49	1.21	1.56	1.16	1.62	1.10	1.70
38	1.33	1.44	1.28	1.50	1.23	1.56	1.17	1.62	1.12	1.70
39	1.34	1.44	1.29	1.50	1.24	1.56	1.19	1.63	1.13	1.69
40	1.35	1.45	1.30	1.51	1.25	1.57	1.20	1.63	1.15	1.69
45	1.39	1.48	1.34	1.53	1.30	1.58	1.25	1.63	1.21	1.69
50	1.42	1.50	1.38	1.54	1.34	1.59	1.30	1.64	1.26	1.69
55	1.45	1.52	1.41	1.56	1.37	1.60	1.33	1.64	1.30	1.69
60	1.47	1.54	1.44	1.57	1.40	1.61	1.37	1.65	1.33	1.69
65	1.49	1.55	1.46	1.59	1.43	1.62	1.40	1.66	1.36	1.69
70	1.51	1.57	1.48	1.60	1.45	1.63	1.42	1.66	1.39	1.70
75	1.53	1.58	1.50	1.61	1.47	1.64	1.45	1.67	1.42	1.70
80	1.54	1.59	1.52	1.62	1.49	1.65	1.47	1.67	1.44	1.70
85	1.56	1.60	1.53	1.63	1.51	1.65	1.49	1.68	1.46	1.71
90	1.57	1.61	1.55	1.64	1.53	1.66	1.50	1.69	1.48	1.71
95	1.58	1.62	1.56	1.65	1.54	1.67	1.52	1.69	1.50	1.71
100	1.59	1.63	1.57	1.65	1.55	1.67	1.53	1.70	1.51	1.72

SOURCE: J. Durbin and G. S. Watson, "Testing for Serial Correlation in Least Squares Regression," *Biometrika*, Vol. 38 (1951), pp. 159-177. Reprinted with the permission of the authors.

REFERENCES

Allen, R. G. D., *Mathematical Economics*. New York: Macmillan, 1956.

Ando, Albert, and Modigliani, Franco, "The 'Life Cycle' Hypothesis of Saving: Aggregate Implications and Test," *American Economic Review*, Vol. 53, pp. 55-84 (March 1963).

Brown, T. W., "Habit Persistence and Lags in Consumer Behavior," *Econometrica*, Vol. 20, pp. 355-371 (July 1952).

Cagan, Phillip, "The Monetary Dynamics of Hyperinflation," in *Studies in the Quantity Theory of Money*, Milton Friedman, ed. Chicago: University of Chicago Press, 1956.

Christ, Carl, *Econometric Models and Methods*. New York: Wiley, 1968.

Cobb, C. W., and Douglas, P. H., "A Theory of Production," *American Economic Review*, Vol. 18, pp. 139-165 (May 1928).

Consumer Buying Prospects, Vol. 1, No. 1. Baltimore: Commercial Credit Co., 1966.

de Janosi, P. E., *Factors Influencing the Demand for New Automobiles: A Cross-Section Analysis*. Doctoral dissertation, Ann Arbor: University of Michigan, 1956.

de Leeuw, Frank, and Gramlich, Edward, "The Federal Reserve—MIT Econometric Model," *Federal Reserve Bulletin*, Vol. 54, pp. 11-40 (1968).

Dean, J., "Statistical Cost Functions of a Hosiery Mill," *Journal of Business of the University of Chicago*, Vol. 14, pp. 1-116 (1941).

Douglas, P. H., "Are There Laws of Production?" *American Economic Review*, Vol. 38, pp. 1-41 (May 1948).

Draper, N. R., and Smith, H., *Applied Regression Analysis*. New York: Wiley, 1968.

163

References

Duesenberry, James S., *Income, Saving, and the Theory of Consumer Behavior.* Cambridge: Harvard University Press, 1952.

Duesenberry, James S., Fromm, G., Klein, L. R., and Kuh, E., *The Brookings Quarterly Econometric Model of the United States.* Chicago: Rand McNally, 1965.

Durbin, J., "A Note on Regression When There is Extraneous Information about One of the Coefficients," *Journal of the American Statistical Association*, Vol. 48, pp. 799–808 (December 1953).

Durbin, J., "Estimation of Parameters in Time-Series Regression Models," *Journal of the Royal Statistical Society*, Vol. 22, Series B, pp. 139–153 (1960).

Durbin, J., and Watson, G. S., "Testing for Serial Correlation in Least Squares Regression I," *Biometrika*, Vol. 37, pp. 409–428 (December 1950).

Durbin, J., and Watson, G. S., "Testing for Serial Correlation in Least Squares Regression II," *Biometrika*, Vol. 38, pp. 159–178 (June 1951).

Evans, M. K., and Klein, L. R., *The Wharton Econometric Forecasting Model.* Philadelphia: University of Pennsylvania Press, 1967.

Farrar, D. E., and Glauber, R. R., "Multicollinearity in Regression Analysis: The Problem Revisited," *Review of Economics and Statistics*, Vol. 49, pp. 92–107 (February 1967).

Feldstein, M. S., *Economic Analysis of Health Service Efficiency.* Amsterdam: North-Holland, 1967.

Fox, Karl A., *The Analysis of Demand for Farm Products*, Technical Bulletin No. 1081. Washington: U.S. Department of Agriculture, 1953.

Fox, Karl A., *Econometric Analysis for Public Policy.* Ames: Iowa State University Press, 1958.

Friedman, M., *A Theory of the Consumption Function.* Princeton: Princeton University Press, 1957.

Fuller, Wayne A., and Martin, James E., "The Effects of Autocorrelated Errors in the Statistical Estimation of Distributed Lag Models," *Journal of Farm Economics*, Vol. 41, pp. 71–82 (January 1961).

Girshick, Meyer A., and Haavelmo, Trygve, "Statistical Analysis of the Demand for Food: Examples of Simultaneous Estimation of Structural Equations," *Econometrica*, Vol. 15, pp. 79–116 (April 1947).

Goldberger, Arthur S., *Impact Multipliers and Dynamic Properties of the Klein–Goldberger Model.* Amsterdam: North-Holland, 1959.

Goldberger, Arthur S., *Econometric Theory.* New York: Wiley, 1964.

Goldberger, Arthur S., *Topics in Regression Analysis.* New York: Macmillan, 1968.

Griliches, Zvi, "Distributed Lags: A Survey," *Econometrica*, Vol. 35, pp. 16–49 (January 1967).

Hu, T. W., Lee, M. L., and Stromsdorfer, E. W., "Economic Returns to Vocational and Comprehensive High School Graduates," *Journal of Human Resources*, pp. 25–50 (Winter 1971).

Johnston, J., *Statistical Cost Analysis.* New York: McGraw-Hill, 1960.

Johnston, J., *Econometric Methods.* New York: McGraw-Hill, 1963.

Keynes, J. M., *The General Theory of Employment, Interest, and Money.* New York: Harcourt Brace, 1936.

Klein, L. R., *Economic Fluctuations in the United States, 1921–1941*, Cowles Commission Monograph 11. New York: Wiley, 1950.

Klein, L. R., "The Estimation of Distributed Lags," *Econometrica*, Vol. 26, pp. 553-565 (October 1958).

Klein, L. R., *An Introduction to Econometrics.* Englewood Cliffs: Prentice-Hall, 1962.

Koopmans, T. C., Rubin, H., and Leipnik, R. B., "Measuring the Equation Systems of Dynamic Economics," chap. 2 in *Statistical Inference in Dynamic Economic Models*, Cowles Commission Monograph 10, T. C. Koopmans, ed. New York: Wiley, 1950, pp. 53–237.

Koyck, L., *Distributed Lags and Investment Analysis.* Amsterdam: North-Holland, 1954.

Lee, Maw Lin, "An Analysis of Installment Borrowing by Durable Goods Buyers," *Econometrica*, Vol. 30, pp. 770-787 (October 1962).

Liebenberg, M., Hirsh, A., and Hopkin, J., "A Quarterly Econometric Model of the United States: A Progress Re-

References

port," *Survey of Current Business*, Vol. 46, pp. 13–39 (1966).

Moore, H. L., *Economic Cycles: Their Law and Cause.* New York: Macmillan, 1914.

Nerlove, Marc, *Distributed Lags and Demand Analysis for Agricultural and Other Commodities*, Washington: U. S. Department of Agriculture, 1958(a).

Nerlove, Marc, *The Dynamics of Supply: Estimation of Farmers' Response to Price.* Baltimore: Johns Hopkins University Press, 1958(b).

Samuelson, Paul, *Economics: An Introductory Analysis.* New York: McGraw-Hill, 1969.

Sargan, J. D., "The Estimation of Economic Relationships Using Instrumental Variables," *Econometrica*, Vol. 26, pp. 393–415 (July 1958).

Schultz, H., *The Theory and Measurement of Demand.* Chicago: The University of Chicago Press, 1938.

Stone, Richard, "The Analysis of Market Demand," *Journal of Royal Statistical Society*, Vol. 108, pp. 286–382 (1945).

Stone, Richard, *The Measurement of Consumers' Expenditure and Behavior in the United Kingdom, 1928–1938.* Cambridge: Cambridge University Press, 1954.

Suits, Daniel B., "The Demand for New Automobiles in the United States 1929-1956," *Review of Economics and Statistics*, pp. 273–281 (August 1958).

Theil, H., "Estimation and Simultaneous Correlation in Complete Equation Systems," The Hague: Centraal Planbureau, 1953.

Tinbergen, J., *Statistical Testing of Business Cycle Theories, II.* Geneva: League of Nations, 1939.

Tobin, J., "A Statistical Demand Function for Food in the U.S.A.," *Journal of Royal Statistical Society*, Vol. 113, pp. 113–141 (1950).

Tobin, J., "Estimation of Relationships for Limited Dependent Variables," *Econometrica*, Vol. 26, pp. 24–36 (January 1958).

Wald, A., "The Fitting of Straight Lines If Both Variables Are Subject to Error," *Annual of Mathematical Statistics*, Vol. 11, pp. 284–300 (1940).

Walsh, R. M., "Response to Price in the Production of Cotton and Cottonseed," *Journal of Farm Economics*, Vol. 26, pp. 359–372 (August 1940).

Wold, H. O. A., and Jureen, L., *Demand Analysis.* New York: Wiley, 1953.

Working, Elmer J., "What Do Statistical Demand Curves Show?" *Quarterly Journal of Economics*, Vol. 41, pp. 212–235 (February 1927).

Zellner, Arnold, "The Short-Run Consumption Function," *Econometrica*, Vol. 25, pp. 552–567 (October 1957).

Zellner, Arnold, and Theil, H., "Three-Stage Least Squares: Simultaneous Estimation of Simultaneous Equations," *Econometrica*, Vol. 30, pp. 54–78 (January 1962).

INDEX

Index

Duesenberry, J., 116
Durbin-Watson statistics, 79–80

Endogenous variables, 121
Engel curves, 61
Errors in variables, 85–90
Exogenous variables, 121
Expectation (E), 9
  coefficient of, 92
Extraneous information estimation, 76

F distribution, 29–30
Feldstein, M., 108
Fox, K. A., 100, 143–144
Friedman, M., 88, 117
Full-information maximum likelihood method, 141–142
Fuller, W., 94
Functional form, 60–62
  choice of, 62–65

Generalized least-squares method, 84, 142
Girshick, M. A., 142
Goldberger, A. S., 57, 59, 76, 95, 127, 135, 138, 139, 141
Griliches, Z., 95

Haavelmo, T., 142
Heteroscedasticity, 82–85
Hypotheses testing, 25–29, 47–48

Identification, 128–135
Identified relation, 133–135
Independent variables, 60
Indirect least-squares method, 135–137
Instrumental variable method, 88–89, 139
Interval estimation, 20–23

Johnston, J., 42, 46, 59, 90, 111–113

Keynesian model, 116, 121–126
Klein, L. R., 95, 145
Koopmans, T. C., 141
Koyck, L., 92

Lagged variables, 90–95
Least variance ratio method, 140

170